Reading & Writing *Excellence*

KEYS TO STANDARDS-BASED ASSESSMENT

Estelle Kleinman

STECK-VAUGHN
BERRENT
A Harcourt Company

www.steck-vaughn.com

ACKNOWLEDGMENTS

Project Author:	Estelle Kleinman	**Art Director:**	Frank Bruno
Executive Editor:	Carol Traynor	**Design and Production:**	Susan Geer Associates, Inc.
Senior Editor:	Amy Losi	**Designer I:**	Julene Mays
Editor II:	Caren Churchbuilder	**Design Associate:**	Gregory Silverman
Editor I:	Edward Nasello	**Cover Design:**	S. Michelle Wiggins
Associate Editor:	Christy Yaros	**Photo Research:**	Sarah Fraser
Assistant to the		**Illustrators:**	Alex DeLange
Editorial Dept. :	Virginia Giustino		Seitu Hayden
Project Consultant:	Howard Berrent		Holly Jones
			Tim Jones

Steck-Vaughn/Berrent is indebted to the following for permission to use material in this book:

page 9 "Ride the Indian" – Reprinted by permission of CRICKET magazine, February 2000, Vol. 27, No. 6, © 2000 by Andrew T. Pelletier.

page 23 "Close Encounters of the Bear Kind" by Susan E. Quinlan from Muse Magazine, November 2000. Reprinted by permission of Susan E. Quinlan.

page 30 "After a Volcano Erupts" by Sharlene P. Nelson. Copyright © 1999 by Highlights for Children, Inc., Columbus, Ohio.

page 34 "A Ghostly Game of Puckeen" – Reprinted by permission of CRICKET magazine, October 1999, Vol. 27, No.2, © 1999 by Kathleen M. Muldoon.

page 38 "Living near Lions" by Cecil Dzwowa. Copyright © 2000 by Highlights for Children, Inc., Columbus, Ohio.

page 46 "Drilling in the Ocean Floor" by Jack Myers. Copyright © 2000 by Highlights for Children, Inc., Columbus, Ohio.

page 58 "Thingyan: New Year in Myanmar" by Marci Stillerman. Copyright © 2000 by Highlights for Children, Inc., Columbus, Ohio.

page 64 "Raccoon Summer" – Reprinted by permission of CRICKET magazine, July 2000, Vol. 27, No. 11, © 2000 by Mary L. Johnson.

page 70 "Blast to the Past" by Michael N. Smith/NGS Image Collection from National Geographic World, February 2001. Reprinted by permission of National Geographic Society.

page 90 "Stand Like a Trumpet" – Reprinted by permission of CRICKET magazine, July 1999, Vol. 26, No. 11, © 1999 by Deborah J. Rasmussen.

page 106 "Star-Spangled Seamstress" by Lynn E. McElfresh. Copyright © 2000 by Highlights for Children, Inc., Columbus, Ohio.

page 120 "Flying Trains" – Reprinted by permission of CRICKET magazine, February 2000, Vol. 27, No. 6, © 2000 by Pam Daniels.

Photo Credits:
Cover photo: John Wang/©PhotoDisc p.23; ©Fred Whitehead/Animals Animals; p.25 ©Johnny Johnson/Animals Animals; p.30 ©CORBIS; p.38 ©R.S. Virdee/Grant Heilman; p.46 ©Daniel Hulshizer/AP/Wide World, Inc.; p.59 ©Alison Wright/CORBIS; p.76 ©Lake County Museum/CORBIS; p.106 Courtesy, American Antiquarian Society; p.120 ©Michael S. Yamashia/CORBIS.

Table of Contents

Students are instructed to approach a selection and test question using the **Four *R*s:** **R**eady, **R**ead, **R**espond, **R**eview.

Unit 1 introduces the three levels of comprehension—literal, interpretive, and critical—and presents specific strategies designed to assist students in answering multiple-choice and short-answer questions. Each question is identified in the instruction by the type of skill it covers.

Unit 2 explains how students can use graphic organizers to help them answer essay questions. A graphic organizer accompanies each of six selections. Students are given instruction in how to use the different organizers to answer essay questions about the selections. Each question is identified in the instruction by the type of skill it covers.

Unit 3 builds upon what was taught in the previous two units. Students apply what they have learned to answer multiple-choice and open-ended questions about various selections. There are hints to help them answer each question. Each question is identified in the hint by the type of skill it covers.

Unit 4 provides students with an opportunity to independently practice the strategies they have learned. This unit may be used as a test to assess students' learning and to simulate formal tests.

To the Teacher

Reading & Writing Excellence is a series of instructional books designed to prepare students to take standardized reading tests. It introduces the **Four *R*s,** a strategy that will enable students to read selections, understand what they have read, and answer multiple-choice and open-ended questions about the reading material. Special emphasis is given to using graphic organizers as prewriting aids for answering essay questions.

Many genres, such as fiction, nonfiction, poems, fables, and folk tales are included. Many of the passages are taken from published literature, reflecting the type of instruction that exists in classrooms today. The questions accompanying each passage represent the different levels of comprehension.

The material in this book provides your students with step-by-step instruction that will maximize their reading success in classroom work as well as in testing situations.

The Four *R*s to Success

When you approach any kind of a task, it helps to start with a plan. A plan provides you with the specific steps you must follow to accomplish your goal.

When you take a reading test, you need a plan that will help you understand a selection and answer questions about it. You can follow this plan by remembering the **Four *R*s: R**eady, **R**ead, **R**espond, **R**eview.

Ready Before you read, you need to get ready.

▶ **Set a purpose for reading** Think about why you are reading. This will help you to focus. If you are reading to answer questions for a test, you will be looking for information. You will also be reading to understand how the different parts of the selection fit together.

▶ **Preview the selection** Try to find out as much about the selection as you can before you read it. Read the title, flip through the pages, glance at any illustrations or diagrams, and read any headings. You might also want to skim the first paragraph.

▶ **Make predictions** Next, predict what you will find in the text.

Read The next step is to read the selection. You will better understand what you read if you take an active role.

▶ **Anticipate what will follow** Continue to make predictions as you work your way through the text. For works of fiction, ask yourself, "What will happen next?" For nonfiction selections, try to figure out what the next part of the selection will be about.

▶ **Monitor your own understanding** As you read, ask yourself questions about things you might not understand. Take the time to speculate about answers to your questions. Then, reread parts of the selection to determine if your answers are correct.

▶ **Confirm your predictions** Keep your predictions in mind as you read. Are things turning out the way you expected? Make new predictions as you acquire more information. Continue the process until you have finished the selection.

Respond
Now you are ready to answer some questions about the selection.

▶ **Read the question**   Read each question carefully. For multiple-choice questions, be sure to read each of the choices as well.

▶ **Think about it**   Think about which parts of the selection will help you figure out the answer. Reread those sections. For multiple-choice questions, have the choices in mind as you do this. For open-ended questions, be sure to organize your thoughts before you begin to write your answer.

▶ **Answer the question**   You are now ready to answer the question. For multiple-choice questions, more than one answer often sounds right. Be careful to choose the *best* answer. If you are writing your answer, make sure to include all the points you want to make.

Review
Take another look at your answer. Did you pick the best choice for your multiple-choice question? Did you answer all parts of your open-ended question? Does your answer make sense? Be sure to check your spelling, punctuation, and grammar.

• • •

Three Levels of Comprehension

In this unit you will learn how to answer questions at three "key" levels of comprehension.

LEVEL 1: *Find the Key* (Literal Level)

Look for information—At the literal level, you recall or recognize information. The information you need is stated right in the selection.

LEVEL 2: *Turn the Lock* (Interpretive Level)

Determine meaning—At the interpretive level, you use the information in the selection to figure out the answers to questions. You might be explaining meaning. Or, you might be using clues to draw conclusions. For this level, you must show that you understand the information in the selection. You must also know how the different parts fit together.

LEVEL 3: *Open the Door* (Critical Level)

Go beyond the text—At the critical level, you think about the selection and add what you know from your own experiences. You evaluate and extend meaning. You also make judgments about what you have read.

LEVEL 1: Find the Key
Introduction to Literal Questions

A literal question will ask you to recall or recognize information. The answer to the question is found in the selection.

Types of literal questions may include the following:

► Identifying details from the selection
► Identifying the order of events
► Identifying cause and effect situations
► Identifying character traits

Identify key words

The key to answering a literal question is to find out where the answer is located. Think about where the information might appear in the selection. Then identify key words in the question that might also appear in the selection. For example, look at the following question:

Which storms are most destructive in the United States?

To answer this question, you would look for the key words *storms, destructive,* and *United States.* If you cannot find these words, look for words that mean about the same thing. Instead of *destructive,* for example, you might look for *harmful* or *deadly.* Or, you might look for examples of destruction, such as *loss of life* or *property damage.*

Find the clues

Sometimes you will not have key words to help you. Then you must think carefully about what the question is asking. Look at this question:

Which sentence states the main idea of the passage?

Here there are no key words to look for, but the answer can still be found in the selection. First, you must know that the *main idea* is the central idea in the passage. So you would look for the one sentence that clearly tells what the whole selection is about.

Answering Literal Questions

Now you will learn how to answer literal questions about a story. Be sure to follow the **Four *R*s:**

4Rs

Ready—Get ready to read

Read—Read the selection

Respond—Answer the question

Review—Check your answer

DIRECTIONS: Read this story about an unusual motorcycle. Then answer questions I through 8.

Ride the Indian

by Andrew T. Pelletier

A long time ago in a little country town, there was a boy who liked to tinker and invent things. He knew all about engines and he could fix anything that moved. He was the first person in town to own a motorcycle and he had to go all the way to the city to get it. It was an Indian motorcycle with spoked wheels, a shiny leather seat, and an engine so small that you had to look closely to see that it wasn't a bicycle.

The boy's name was Franklin Boggs, and he was a bit of a daredevil. He liked nothing better than to speed down the main street or along the dusty back roads, chasing chickens back to their farms. He liked to race the Indian along the cow paths on the hills overlooking town, and whenever people heard the whine of his engine and saw him flying along in his long white scarf and leather helmet, they shook their heads and smiled and said, "There goes Frank—he thinks he's one of the Wright brothers!"

Frank kept that motorcycle in perfect condition. He gassed it up and oiled it and tinkered with the engine and wiped down the brown leather seat after every ride. His little nephew, Jack Boggs, sat nearby and watched whenever Frank was

tinkering with the Indian. "I always keep her oiled up and ready to go!" Frank would say. "I never know when I might want to take a spin!"

In 1917, the United States entered the Great War that was going on over in Europe, and Frank joined the army. The day he left he took one last ride through town. Then he wheeled the motorcycle into the back of the dark toolshed and hung his leather helmet over the handlebars. Before leaving, he asked Jack to take care of the Indian until he came home again, and Jack promised that he would. Frank then put on his tin army helmet and picked up his duffel bag and headed off for the train station.

Frank sent Jack a letter every week, and every letter ended the same way: "Take care of the Indian! I never know when I might want to take a spin!"

But then the letters stopped. Frank never came home from the war.

Jack Boggs grew up to be a tinkerer and fix-it man, just like Frank. He always took good care of the Indian, just as he had promised. Once a week he wheeled it out of the toolshed and into the sunny barnyard. He checked the oil and wiped down the seat and put in a few drops of gas. He turned over the engine just to make sure that it was running well, but he never rode the Indian. "I wouldn't feel right," he'd say if anyone asked. "I promised Frank I'd keep it in good shape, and what if something bad happened?" Then he would roll the motorcycle back into the shed.

Seventy years went by, and Jack grew old. He wasn't feeling well, and it was hard for him to get around. So one day he brought his own grandson, who was also named Franklin Boggs, into the back of the cluttered old shed and showed him the Indian. He told young Franklin the story of the motorcycle and asked the boy to take over the job of caring for it. Franklin promised that he would.

Once a week, when he got home from school, Franklin went to the toolshed and rolled the Indian out into the barnyard. He put it up onto its kickstand and checked the oil. Once in a while he put a few drops of gasoline into the tank. He took a soft cloth and some more oil and cleaned and shined the seat and the old leather helmet until both looked like new. When he was finished, the Indian looked so good that Franklin couldn't help but climb up onto the seat, put on the helmet and the old white scarf that he had found in the attic, and pretend that he was racing along the cow paths high above town. Finally he pushed the starter, and the motorcycle roared to life. Franklin really, really wanted to go for a ride, but he, too, had made a promise. "It just doesn't seem right," he said to himself. "What if something bad happened?" He shut down the engine, climbed off, and rolled the Indian back into the shed.

One night, after he had finished taking care of the Indian, Franklin had a hard time falling asleep. There was a full moon that night. It made him restless and kept him tossing and turning. When he finally did drift off, he had a strange and vivid dream. In the dream he heard the sound of the Indian's engine roaring to life down in the barnyard, and then he saw the motorcycle speed down the driveway and up the road. On it rode a dark figure trailing a long white scarf. The sound of the engine echoed far down the valley and high on the cow paths overlooking town, and the headlight beam bounced and danced crazily over the dark landscape.

The hum of the motorcycle drifted farther and farther away, the headlight beam grew fainter and fainter, and then the dream was over.

In the morning, as soon as the first daylight poked over the barn roof and into Franklin's bedroom, he awoke with a start. He suddenly remembered the dream, so he sprang up and rushed out to the toolshed. The Indian was still there, looking just as he had left it. The seat was shiny and clean, and the gas tank was full to the brim. He gave a great sigh of relief and turned to go back to the house. But just as he was about to flip off the light, he noticed something very odd. The old motorcycle helmet, the leather one that had hung from the handlebars for all those years, was gone. In its place was a rusty, old, tin army helmet. And scrawled in the thick dust that coated the helmet, he could make out some words written in a quavering, old-fashioned hand.

"Thank you for remembering," Franklin read. "Ride the Indian!"

DIRECTIONS: Read each question carefully. Darken the circle at the bottom of the page or write your answer on the lines.

1 The first Franklin Boggs is described as—

   A a genius

   B a daredevil

   C a villain

   D an eccentric

Find the Key

This question asks you to identify details from the story. Read the question and the choices carefully. You must choose the correct answer from among the four choices. The answer to this question is right in the story. Think about where the answer might be found. Would it appear at the beginning, in the middle, or at the end? What word is used to describe Franklin when the narrator introduces him?

2 What did Jack say he would do while Frank was at war?

   F He would write to Frank every week.

   G He would learn to ride a motorcycle.

   H He would do his best in school.

   J He would care for the Indian.

Find the Key

Here you must also identify details. When you go back to the story to find the answer, look for the key word *told*. If you cannot find this word, look for words that mean about the same thing. Then reread the paragraph that contains these words and the few paragraphs that follow, until you find what Jack said he would do.

Answers

1 Ⓐ Ⓑ Ⓒ Ⓓ   **2** Ⓕ Ⓖ Ⓗ Ⓙ

3 The boxes show some events from the story.

Jack's grandson Franklin starts the Indian.		The old motorcycle helmet is gone.
1	2	3

Which event belongs in Box 2?

A Franklin dreams that someone rode the Indian.

B Jack takes care of the Indian for his Uncle Frank.

C Franklin takes over caring for the Indian from his grandfather.

D Jack's Uncle Frank goes off to war.

Find the Key

This question asks you to identify the sequence of events in the story. Go back to the story and locate the events that appear in the first and third boxes. Then read each choice to see which event occurs *between* these two.

4 Why does neither Jack nor his grandson ride the Indian?

F They think it is against the law to ride someone else's motorcycle.

G They know that the motorcycle is not in very good condition.

H They fear something bad might happen to the motorcycle.

J They do not think that Frank would want them to ride it.

Find the Key

Identify details from the story. Start by eliminating any answers that you know are wrong. Then, to find the right answer, reread the parts of the story where Jack and Franklin give their reasons for not riding the motorcycle. Which choice matches what both of the characters say?

Answers

3 Ⓐ Ⓑ Ⓒ Ⓓ	4 Ⓕ Ⓖ Ⓗ Ⓙ

5 How is Frank's army helmet different from his motorcycle helmet?

_____

_____

_____

_____

Find the Key

This question asks you to contrast two things in the story. The answer is right in the story. Now, instead of choosing an answer, you will be writing your own answer to a question. Read the question carefully. Find the part of the story where Frank goes off to war. Look for a description of each helmet. How are they different? Write your answer in a complete sentence.

6 How is the adult Jack like his Uncle Frank?

_____

_____

_____

_____

Find the Key

This question asks you to identify character traits. Find the section of the story in which the two men are compared. Look for words that indicate a comparison, such as _like_, _similar to_, and _alike_. How does Jack take after his Uncle Frank? Be sure to write your answer in a complete sentence.

7 What does Franklin see in his "strange and vivid dream"?

_____

_____

_____

_____

Find the Key

This question asks you to identify details from the story. Reread the part of the story that tells about Franklin's dream. The words in quotation marks—*strange and vivid dream*—are key words that will help you find this section of the story. Then, tell what he dreams about in a sentence or two.

8 What does the character who left the old army helmet want Franklin to do?

_____

_____

_____

_____

Find the Key

Identify details from the story. The answer is right in the story. Look back to the section where Franklin finds the tin army helmet. Who do you think left this helmet? What does this character want Franklin to do? Be sure to write your answer in a complete sentence.

LEVEL 2: Turn the Lock
Introduction to Interpretive Questions

To solve a mystery, a detective puts together clues to determine the guilty party. When you answer an interpretive question, you put together different pieces of information from a selection to determine meaning.

Types of interpretive questions may include the following:

► Interpreting character traits

► Interpreting vocabulary

► Determining the main idea

► Summarizing information

► Drawing conclusions

Unlock the answer

To answer an interpretive question, you must become a detective. Before a detective can look for clues, he or she must know what to look for. You can tell what to look for by examining the question.

Suppose you had to answer a question about a chapter from *The Adventures of Tom Sawyer* by Mark Twain. In the chapter, young Tom tricks his friends into helping him paint a fence. Look at the following question:

**What character traits help Tom convince
his friends to help him paint the fence?**

The narrator or another person in a work of fiction might tell you what a character is like. More often, however, you will have to infer the character's traits by looking carefully at what he or she thinks, says, and does. What sections of the chapter might you reread to help you? You could look at the conversations that Tom has with his friends. You could also consider Tom's actions and what he is thinking while he carries out his scheme.

Put the clues together

After you have reread parts of the selection, think about what you have read. Then, like a detective, put the clues together to draw a conclusion.

For the question above, you might find that Tom is clever, imaginative, and manipulative. All of these traits help Tom trick his friends.

Answering Interpretive Questions

Now you will learn how to answer interpretive questions about a poem. Remember to follow the **Four Rs:**

4Rs

Ready—Get ready to read

Read—Read the selection

Respond—Answer the question

Review—Check your answer

DIRECTIONS: **Read this poem about Pocahontas, the Native American princess who saved the life of Captain John Smith when he was sentenced to die by her father, Chief Powhatan. Then answer questions 1 through 6.**

Pocahontas

by William Makepeace Thackeray

Wearied arm and broken sword
    Wage in vain the desperate fight;
Round him press a countless **horde,**
    He is but a single knight.
Hark! a cry of triumph shrill
    Through the wilderness *resounds,*
    As, with twenty bleeding wounds,
Sinks the warrior, fighting still.

Now they heap the funeral **pyre,**
    And the torch of death they light;
Ah! 'tis hard to die by fire!
    Who will shield the captive knight?

horde: a large, moving crowd
pyre: a pile of wood

Round the stake with fiendish cry
  Wheel and dance the savage crowd,
  Cold the victim's **mien** and proud,
And his breast is bared to die.

Who will shield the fearless heart?
  Who avert the murderous blade?
From the throng with sudden start
  See, there springs an Indian maid.
Quick she stands before the knight:
"Loose the chain, unbind the ring!
  I am daughter of the king,
And I claim the Indian right!"

Dauntlessly aside she flings
  Lifted axe and thirsty knife,
Fondly to his heart she clings,
  And her bosom guards his life!
In the woods of Powhatan,
  Still 'tis told by Indian fires
  How a daughter of their sires
Saved a captive Englishman.

mien: manner and appearance

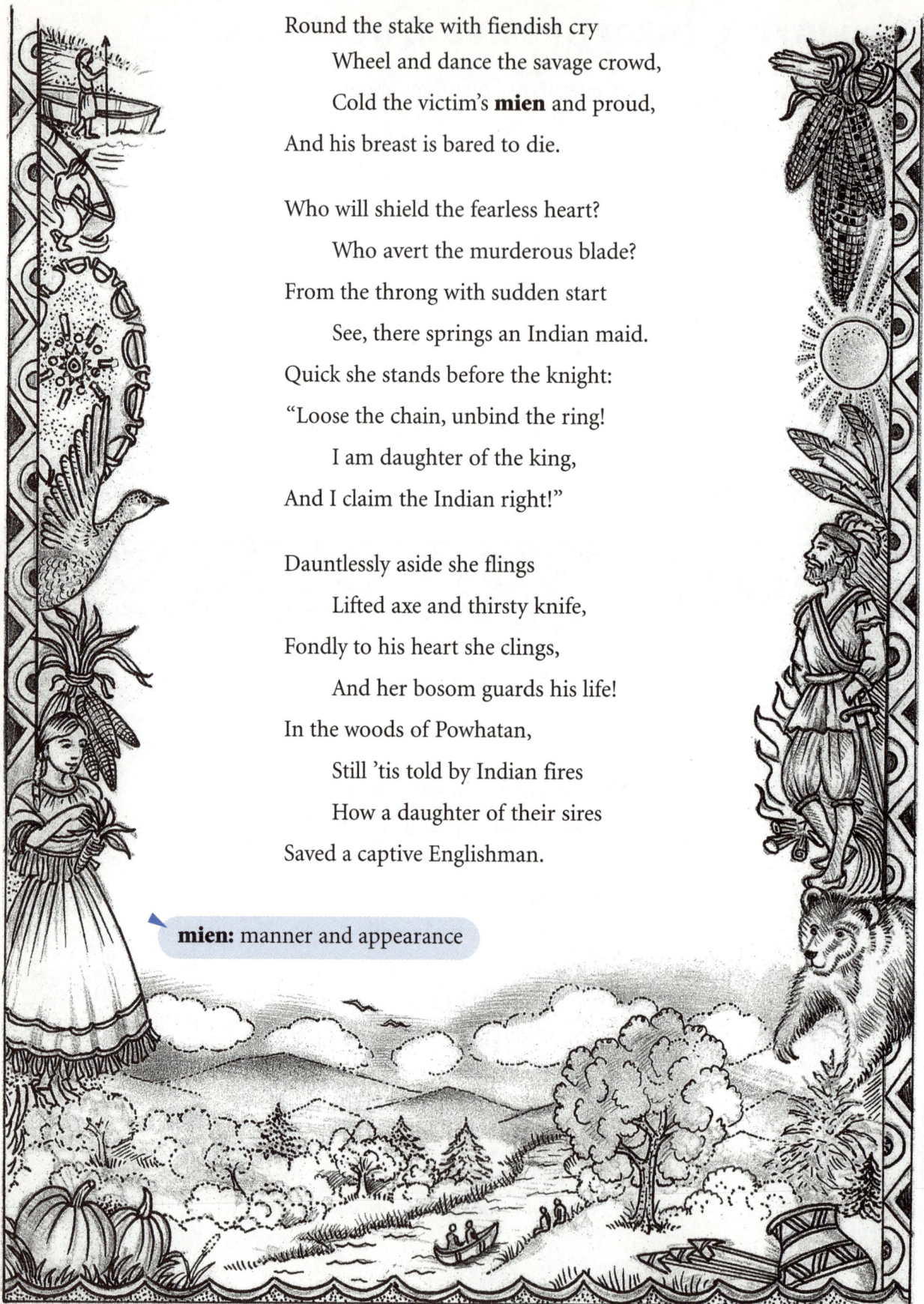

DIRECTIONS: Read each question carefully. Darken the circle at the bottom of the page or write your answer on the lines.

I   In the poem, the word *resounds* means—

   A   vanishes

   B   remains

   C   hesitates

   D   echoes

Turn the Lock

This is a vocabulary question. The word *resounds* may be new to you, but you can figure it out from context. Reread the stanza that contains the word. Does this give you any clues to the word's meaning? What would most likely happen to a shrill cry in the wilderness?

2   Which pair of words *best* describes Pocahontas?

   F   Impulsive and charming

   G   Reckless and resourceful

   H   Courageous and kindhearted

   J   Innocent and dependent

Turn the Lock

This question asks you to determine character traits by choosing a pair of words that describes Pocahontas. You will *not* find the answer in the poem. When choosing an answer, remember that *both* words must pertain to the Indian princess. Think about what Pocahontas does in the poem. What does this tell you about her character? Also, consider how she acts toward the captive John Smith.

Answers

1 Ⓐ Ⓑ Ⓒ Ⓓ	2 Ⓕ Ⓖ Ⓗ Ⓙ

3 Why are the Indians able to capture John Smith?

    A They fight better than he does.

    B They run faster than he does.

    C He is outnumbered.

    D He falls into a trap.

Turn the Lock

This question asks you to draw a conclusion. To figure out the answer to this question, think about the information in the poem. What kind of a fighter is John Smith? Does the poem tell you anything about the weapons used by Smith and the Indians? Is there any mention of how many Indians go against Smith? Is there any indication that he fell into a trap? Reread any sections of the poem that will help you find the answers to these questions.

4 Which characteristic of poetry does this poem display?

    F refrain

    G rhyme

    H metaphor

    J jargon

Turn the Lock

This question asks you to determine a characteristic of this poem. To answer this question, you must know what each term means. A refrain is a line or group of lines repeated at regular intervals. Rhyme is the repetition of the same or similar sounds in words that appear near each other. A metaphor compares two different things. And jargon is slang associated with a particular career or field of study. Look back at the poem and see which choice applies.

Answers

3 Ⓐ Ⓑ Ⓒ Ⓓ	4 Ⓕ Ⓖ Ⓗ Ⓙ

5 What character traits do John Smith and Pocahontas have in common?

_____

_____

_____

_____

Turn the Lock

This question asks you to determine and compare character traits. First look back in the poem to see how John Smith deals with his fight with the Indians and his capture. What traits does he display? Then reread the part of the poem that tells how Pocahontas saves Smith. Does she display any traits similar to those you found for John Smith? What are these?

6 What is the theme of this poem? Explain your answer.

_____

_____

_____

_____

Turn the Lock

A theme is the central idea or message of a literary work. To decide on the theme, think about what happens in the poem. What qualities does Pocahontas display? Does the speaker think these qualities are admirable? What do you think the speaker is trying to say about Pocahontas' deed? What generalization can you make from this?

LEVEL 3: Open the Door
Introduction to Critical Questions

For a critical question, you must go beyond the words on the page. You bring in your own experiences to evaluate, extend meaning, and make judgments about what you have read.

Types of critical questions may include the following:

► Analyzing the situation

► Predicting outcomes

► Determining the author's purpose

► Extending the passage

► Evaluating the passage

Step through the door

Now, you are going to play the role of a judge. Although you will still look for clues to answer a question, now you must also study the information, decide on its importance, and make judgments about it.

Let's go back to the chapter from *The Adventures of Tom Sawyer*. Look at this question:

What do you think should happen to Tom after the chapter ends?

There is no way to find the answer in the story. Even putting together clues will not give you the answer. This question is asking for your opinion. You must base this opinion on what has happened in the story and on your own experiences.

Make a case

A judge never makes a hasty decision, and neither should you. First, consider what you know about the story. To trick the boys, Tom makes painting a fence seem like fun. The boys are so impressed that they bribe Tom to let them do his work for him.

Next, consider how you feel about Tom's actions. Do you see anything wrong with what Tom did? Or, do you think he deserves credit for getting others to do his work?

Now you can make a judgment on what should happen to Tom, based on the story and your feelings about the situation.

Answering Critical Questions

Now you will learn how to answer critical questions about two passages. Don't forget to follow the **Four _R_s:**

4Rs **R**eady—Get ready to read | **R**espond—Answer the question

Read—Read the selection | **R**eview—Check your answer

DIRECTIONS: Read this article about a biologist who studies bear behavior. Next, read the "Bear Safety Tips." Then answer questions 1 and 2.

Close Encounters of the Bear Kind

by Susan Quinlan

Beep . . . . beep . . . . . . beep . . . beep. The quickening beeps of the radio signal tell John Hechtel two things. He's getting close to a bear den and the bear inside is waking up. Bears lower their body temperature less than other hibernators, so they're easily awakened. John and his coworkers crunch loudly as they snowshoe across the crusty snow. Bowed-down branches of willow shrubs weave a carpet of shadows over the snow, making it tough to spot the small breathing hole that usually marks a bear's den. The scientists look carefully and move slowly. It's not a good idea to step on a bear that's just woken up.

John is a biologist with the Alaska Department of Fish and Game. His study area is the Tanana Valley, a boggy lowland in central Alaska. It's prime black bear habitat, but most of the ground is too wet for dens. Unfortunately, the only dry areas that seem good for dens also happen to be used by the U.S. Army for winter training. So to protect both bears and soldiers, the army hired John to find out where most bears in the area hibernate.

John spent last summer fitting bears with radio collars like the one that is now leading him to a den. The collar has a transmitter that sends out a beep John can track to its source. It also has an activity sensor that speeds up the beeps when the bear moves.

John has captured bears in traps made from 55-gallon drums. He's also darted some from the air. Darting a bear from the open door of a helicopter—held in by just a seat belt or climbing harness—sounds challenging. But John says, "No, it's not—if I have a good pilot. If I'm worried about the helicopter rotors getting too close to the treetops, then it is tough to focus. But if I trust the pilot, it's fairly simple. The more difficult part is following the bear afterward. It takes from three to eight minutes for the drug to take full effect. We have to keep close enough to watch the bear without making it panic. If the bear falls into water, then I have to get down right away and make sure its head stays up, so it doesn't drown."

John and his coworkers calmly close in on this sleeping bear. The beeping signal is now strong and fast. John spots a small hole in the snow that he figures may mark the den entrance. Before moving in, he pulls a sleeping bag out of his pack. Holding it in one hand, he advances.

The blinding glare of spring sunlight glinting off the snow makes it tough to make out where the bear is in the hole. John crouches down, shades his eyes with his hands and puts his face close to peer inside. With a startled look, he pulls back and whips the sleeping bag over the hole. The black bear inside is not only awake, its head is right at the entrance. John hopes the sleeping bag will keep the den dark and the bear calm a bit longer. He carefully readies a drug-filled hypodermic needle mounted on a short stick. It will take good aim and a quick jab to poke the needle into the bear's shoulder.

Fortunately John has had practice, so this bear is drugged safely. He and his coworkers then measure the bear and the den. They return the bear to its sleeping hole after a half-hour. Occasionally, they don't return the bear. Instead, they take it to an artificial den at the University of Alaska, where other scientists can study its hibernation more easily.

John has tracked down quite a few bear dens—about 100, he thinks. In most cases, the bear is not so alert and not so near the den entrance. Usually, John must squeeze his broad-shouldered, six-foot-tall frame inside the den, and then, without room to maneuver, jab the tranquilizing needle into the waking bear.

Most people probably wouldn't want this job. But John feels that the chance to climb into the private world of a black bear is a great privilege. After studying North American bears for 20 years, John sees bears differently than most people do. "Bears are not vicious animals to be feared," he says. "I see a lot of the same traits in bears that I see in dogs, and even people—including curiosity and playfulness. Sure, bears sometimes attack, but in nearly all cases there are specific circumstances that explain the bear's behavior. How would you feel if you were sleeping and woke up to see a stranger standing in the room? It's understandable if a surprised bear gets a bit upset."

John's main worry in his work is not his own safety but that of the bears. "I enjoy the opportunity to study and handle bears," he says. "But I also hate to hassle them. It's important to me to be sure the work we are doing is worth what we are putting the bears through . . . But I have learned that we can't just leave bears alone and expect everything to be OK. We have to know more about bears and bear behavior to protect them and their habitats."

Bear Safety Tips

Powerful animals, bears will defend themselves and their territory if threatened. All bears are potentially dangerous. But they are also an important part of the park ecosystem. With your cooperation, bears and people can exist together. Play it smart by following these safety tips.

Camping

You can enjoy a night in the wilderness without attracting bears to your camp.

1. Put away food and garbage.
2. Lock food in the trunk of your vehicle.
3. Do not cook or eat in or near your tent.
4. Clean all utensils and put garbage in closed containers.
5. Use a flashlight at night to warn bears away.

Hiking

Remember that a surprised bear is a dangerous bear.

1. Hike in a group and make loud noises to alert a bear of your presence.
2. Stay in the open whenever possible.
3. Never approach a bear, especially a cub.
4. Avoid berry patches and dead animals, as these are basic food sources for bears.
5. Look for bear signs, diggings, tracks, and droppings.

Bear Encounters

In any close encounter with a bear, keep calm and assess the situation.

1. Leave the area if you see a bear at a distance.
2. Do not run. Stand your ground or back away slowly and diagonally.
3. Do not scream or make a sudden movement.

DIRECTIONS: Read each question carefully. Then write your answer in a paragraph on the lines.

1 Which two of the bear safety tips do you think are most important for John Hechtel to keep in mind while doing his job? Give reasons to support your answer.

_____

_____

_____

_____

_____

_____

_____

Open the Door

This question asks you to make a connection among the two selections and determine relevant information. Review the safety tips on page 25. Consider how Hechtel would use each tip on his job. Think about which ones are the most important to Hechtel and decide why you feel this way. Narrow your choices down to two. Write your answer in a complete paragraph. Start by stating the safety tips you feel are most important for John Hechtel. Then support your answer with details from the selections.

2 Suppose you were writing a letter to the U.S. Fish and Wildlife Service to convince them to spend more money studying bear behavior. Which of the two selections would best help you make your case and why? Use details from the selection to support your answer.

_____

_____

_____

_____

_____

_____

_____

_____

_____

Open the Door

This question asks you to evaluate and extend meaning. Think about the purpose of your letter. Then look at each selection carefully. What support could you find for your argument in the article? Next look at the safety tips. How might they help you make your point? Which group of details would you find most useful in your letter? Why?

Speak Out

Imagine that you are John Hechtel. You are asked to talk to a group of students on Career Day about your job. In your talk, you will tell what you do, what you like about your job, and the safety precautions that you take. Use information from both selections to prepare your speech. Then present it to the class.

Summary

In this unit, you have learned how to answer questions at three "key" levels of comprehension.

Find the Key	*Turn the Lock*	*Open the Door*

"Literal"	**"Interpretive"**	**"Critical"**
Look for information	*Determine meaning*	*Go beyond the text*

Remember that no matter what type of question you answer, you should always use the **Four *R*s: R**eady, **R**ead, **R**espond, **R**eview.

Ready—Get ready to read

▶ Set a purpose for reading
▶ Preview the selection
▶ Make predictions

Read—Read the selection

▶ Anticipate what will follow
▶ Monitor your understanding
▶ Confirm your predictions

Respond—Answer the question

▶ Read the question
▶ Think about it
▶ Answer the question

Review—Check your answer

Graphic Organizers: The Key to Answering Essay Questions

The Essay Question

In Unit 1 you answered both multiple-choice and short-answer questions. Now you will learn how to answer essay questions, for which you will write responses of two or more paragraphs. Essay questions often require more thought and planning than other types of questions.

Get Organized!

You know how difficult it is to find something in a messy drawer. You search and search, but the item you are looking for escapes you in the clutter. However, finding something in a well-organized drawer is very easy. In the same way, you can answer an essay question more easily if you are organized before you begin to write.

A **graphic organizer** is a conceptual frame that allows you to collect ideas and categorize them. It helps you gather the information necessary to answer your essay question. Once you organize your ideas, it will be easier for you to write your essay.

In this unit, you will learn how to use different kinds of graphic organizers to answer essay questions. But first, here are some things to think about before you begin to write.

Before You Write

Before you write anything, ask yourself some questions:

1. *What is my topic?* What will you be writing about? State the topic in a few words. This will help you focus your writing.

2. *Why am I writing?* Think about the purpose of the essay. Usually you write to explain something, persuade someone, entertain someone, or describe something.

3. *Who will read my writing?* Consider who will be your audience. Your teacher will probably be your audience for a test, so you should use a formal tone and be careful to use correct spelling, punctuation, and grammar.

DIRECTIONS: Read the following article about Mount St. Helens. Then you will use a Compare-Contrast Grid. It will help you compare and contrast the area around Mount St. Helens.

After a Volcano Erupts

by Sharlene P. Nelson

For many summers, people visited Mount St. Helens in the southwest part of Washington State. The visitors climbed over the mountain's snowfields and glaciers to its 9,700-foot-high top.

Far below, campers hiked through thick forests of fir and cedar trees. Other people enjoyed catching trout in Spirit Lake at the mountain's base.

Few people knew that Mount St. Helens was a sleeping volcano. It had last erupted more than one hundred years ago. Glaciers and forests had covered the mountain's scars from that eruption.

In March 1980, Mount St. Helens began to show signs that it might erupt again. Earthquakes rumbled beneath the mountain. A blast of steam and rock dust burst from the mountaintop.

Earthquakes and mild explosions continued. Scientists from Vancouver, Washington, set up a camp about five miles from the mountain's top to observe its activity. On May 18, a scientist named David Johnston was at the camp to watch the mountain.

Disaster

Suddenly, at 8:32 A.M. a huge landslide began on the mountain's north side. Johnston shouted into his radio, "Vancouver, Vancouver, this is it!" The landslide left a giant hole in the side of the volcano. Seconds later a sideways, or lateral, eruption blasted from the hole. Hot gases, broken rock, and ash rocketed away at speeds of up to 670 miles per hour. The gases were as hot as 570 degrees Fahrenheit.

Trees flew across ridges. Rocks, debris, and trees crashed into Spirit Lake. The landslide mixed with melted ice and snow. The mixture created mudflows that plunged down rivers, destroying homes, roads, and bridges.

A thick cloud of ash rose sixteen miles into the sky. The eruption continued for more than nine hours. It blew away 1,300 feet of the mountain's top, leaving a huge crater. It destroyed trees as far as sixteen miles away, and it killed hundreds of big animals, such as deer, elk, and bears. Fifty-seven people were killed, including David Johnston.

Days later, scientists entered the silent hills and valleys, which were covered with gray ash. They called this area the "blast zone." It looked as if nothing were alive. The scientists thought it would be many years before life could return. But what they found surprised them.

Life Returns

Pocket gophers and moles poked their noses through the ash. They had been safe in their underground burrows.

Insects and spiders crawled from nests deep inside old logs. Fish swam in nearby mountain lakes. They had been protected by ice that covered the lakes.

Some small trees and wild huckleberry bushes were protected by snow. Bulbs and roots of wild flowers were safe under their covering of dirt.

Rains began to wash away ash, exposing the roots and bulbs. In the summer of 1981, fireweed roots sprouted, and the plants' pink flowers brightened the gray land.

Winds carried spiders and seeds into the blast zone. The seeds sprouted in soil where moles and gophers had mixed good soil from their burrows with ash above. The spiders became food for birds that built nests in dead trees.

Elk wandered into the blast zone to feed on the new plants. Bears came to eat wild huckleberries.

"Living Laboratory"

The mountain and much of the blast zone are now called the Mount St. Helens National Volcanic Monument. Scientists continue studying this "living laboratory," where nature is renewing the land.

Scientists are also watching the volcano rebuild itself with smaller eruptions. Inside the mountain's crater is a mound of rock called a lava dome. It is about 1,000 feet high and looks like a pile of steaming, broken rock. More eruptions have built it higher by adding hot lava from below.

During each of these dome-building eruptions, melted rock, too thick to flow beyond the dome, is squeezed to the surface, where it hardens into rock. The last dome eruption occurred in 1986. Scientists think it might take more than two hundred years for the dome to fill the crater and rebuild the volcano to its old height.

Today, visitors can drive into the monument on a new highway. In the summer they pass hillsides blooming with wild flowers, and they can see where small trees grow— the beginning of a new forest.

At the end of the highway is the Johnston Cascades Volcano Observatory, where visitors can look into the crater from only five miles away. The observatory was named for David Johnston, and it was placed near the spot where he stood the day Mount St. Helens erupted.

Compare-Contrast Grid

A **Compare-Contrast Grid** helps you compare and contrast certain features or characteristics of two things. Each *column* of the grid is labeled on the top with one of the subjects being compared. Each *row* of the grid is labeled on the left with a feature or characteristic being compared and contrasted.

Read the essay question and instructions on page 33.

FEATURE _____   _____

Essay Question: Compare and contrast what the area around Mount St. Helens was like after the volcano erupted in 1980 with what it is like today.

1. You will be comparing and contrasting what the area around Mount St. Helens was like just after the eruption with what it is like today. At the top of the first column, write "After Eruption-1980." At the top of the second column, write "Today."

2. Next, write some features of the things you are comparing and contrasting. You might want to list features such as "vegetation," "wildlife," "land and soil," and "people" in the feature column on the grid.

3. Fill in the grid as you read the story again. Write short phrases that tell about the features named in the grid. For some features, you may have to draw a conclusion based on what you read.

Now that you have filled in the **Compare-Contrast Grid,** use it to answer the essay question at the top of the page. Write your answer on a separate sheet of paper.

Turn the Lock

This question asks you to compare and contrast features of Mount St. Helens by identifying details in the selection. To answer this interpretive question, you must put together different pieces of information from the passage.

Look at the graphic organizer. Use the information you listed to write your essay. Write about the way the area has changed first. Describe how it has remained the same next.

4Rs Don't forget the fourth *R* in the **Four *R*s: R**eady, **R**ead, **R**espond, **Review.** It is now time to review your answer. Make sure that your writing is the best it can be. To do this, use the checklist on page 56.

DIRECTIONS: Read the following Irish folk tale about a young man whose life is changed by some ghosts. Then you will use a Character Traits Map. It will help you describe the main character.

A Ghostly Game of Puckeen

retold by Kathleen M. Muldoon

Once upon a bleak Irish morning, a spindly lad named Jack bade his mother good-bye and set out to seek his destiny. The salty sea mists drenched Jack's flimsy coat as he strode along. By nightfall, he could go no farther. He stopped at a farmhouse that nestled in the shadow of a dark castle. An old man ushered Jack inside and led him to a bench in front of an ample fire. "What is it you're wanting, lad?" asked the farmer.

"Please, sir," said Jack, stifling a yawn. "I will gladly work your fields in the morning for supper and a warm bed tonight."

The farmer rubbed his hands together and paced before the mantel.

"Did you see the castle yonder?"

Jack nodded, one eye open, the other halfway to dreamland.

"I will put you in that castle in front of a fire three times the size of mine. There will be a table with every manner of meat and fish, and a bed as soft as moon cheese. I will lock you in, alone. In the morning, if you are still alive, I will give you a farmhouse and my daughter's hand in marriage, should you fancy her."

Jack bolted upright. "I'll do it, if you send no one to kill me!"

"Not I," the farmer muttered. "'Twas my father's castle. Since his death, no man has spent the night and lived to face the morning. Four have tried."

"Sir, I have nothing of this world except courage," Jack replied.

True to the farmer's word, Jack found himself locked in a large room of the castle. It was lit only by a roaring fire and two candles adorning a heavily laden table.

After feasting on roasted lamb, bread, and cheese, Jack stretched out on the floor before the hearth, intent on sleeping away the night and claiming his fortune in the morning. Before long, however, such a ruckus arose on the ceiling above his head that Jack jumped up, and an icy shiver pulsed down his back.

"I'm falling, falling," Jack heard a voice call. As he looked up, two legs, then a man's body, shoulder, arms, and head oozed through a hole in the ceiling. The parts reassembled themselves into a white-headed figure in a triangular-shaped hat and waistcoat such as Jack's grandfather wore. Before Jack could shout, another spirit of a man appeared and then a third, each more ancient than the one before.

Then, just as Jack thought he could bear no more, the first spirit took a puckeen from his waistcoat and began a furious game with the others, the second and third spirits against the first.

"I say," Jack squeaked. "I say, that's hardly fair, two against one."

Without waiting for a reply, Jack joined the first ghost. They played all night, never exchanging a word, never pausing for rest. As the first sliver of sunrise seeped through the castle windows, Jack slumped onto a chair.

"Rest," he croaked. "Rest." The three spirits stopped their frantic kicking and running and surrounded Jack. The first placed his hand on Jack's shoulder.

"We haven't rested for many years," he said. "Perhaps we can now that we've found someone with courage. The others all died of fright before they could help us."

"I was the farmer's father," he continued. He pointed to the other two spirits. "That was my father, and the eldest my grandfather. None of us has peace because in life we cheated many people. We cannot rest until our wrongs are righted."

Jack shrugged. "What can I do?"

"A white mare waits at the post," said the spirit. "Her saddle-bags are filled with gold and a list of families deserving of our restitution. Ride the countryside until the gold is distributed. When you return, look toward the highest turret of the castle to see the results of your deed."

As the spirit stopped talking, the castle door opened, and in walked the farmer and his beautiful daughter. "You . . . you're alive!" the farmer gasped.

Jack whirled around in his chair. The spirits were gone. Before he even touched the hand of the farmer's daughter, Jack jumped up, ran outside, and leaped onto the mare.

"I'll be back!" he shouted. Jack rode uphill and down, over creeks and rivers, over fences and walls. He delivered the spirits' gifts to the shabbiest cottages in the villages. When at last the saddlebags were empty, Jack took the shortest route back to the castle. He tied the mare to the post, then looked up at the tallest turret just in time to see three snow-white doves soar to the heavens.

The castle door opened, and the farmer's enchanting daughter took Jack's hand and pulled him inside. "Welcome home," she said.

The farmer insisted Jack and his new bride live in the castle beside his farmhouse. There they dwelt happily for the rest of their lives. The spirits had left the puckeen behind, and Jack put it on the mantel to remind him of the value of courage and honesty. And sometimes, on a winter's night, he told his children the story of how he and three spirits once played a ghostly game of puckeen.

Character Traits Map

A **Character Traits Map** helps you organize your thoughts to gain insight into a character's personality traits. In this organizer, the name of the character goes in the center box. A character trait goes in each of the four triangular spaces coming off the center. Then, you follow each trait to the box labeled *Event*. In the box you write an event that illustrates the character trait.

Read the essay question and instructions on page 37.

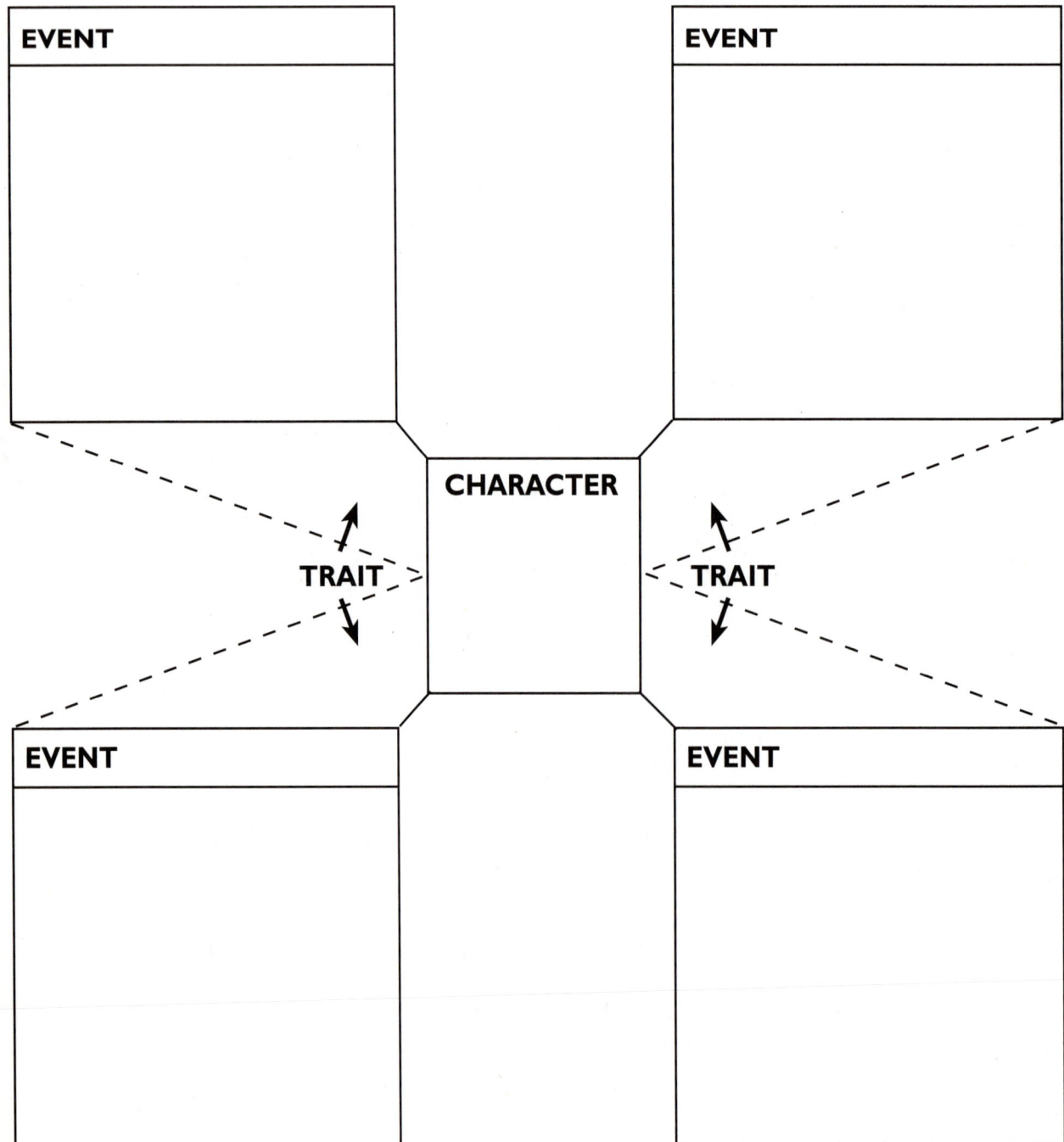

EVENT		EVENT

TRAIT   **CHARACTER**   TRAIT

EVENT		EVENT

Essay Question: Which character trait of Jack's do you think was most important in helping him win the farmhouse and the hand of the farmer's daughter? Which of his character traits was least important? Use details from the story to explain why you chose each word.

1. The question asks you to choose two traits—one that was most important in helping Jack and one that was least important. Since Jack is the character you will be writing about, write his name in the center box of the graphic organizer.

2. Next, think about different character traits that Jack possesses. To help you, look back at the things that he says, thinks, and does. Write a character trait in each of the four spaces.

3. Now follow each of Jack's traits up or down to its "Event" box. Go back to the story to find an event that illustrates the character trait. Then write this event in the box.

Now that you have filled in the **Character Traits Map,** use it to answer the essay question at the top of the page. Write your answer on a separate sheet of paper.

Open the Door

This question asks you to analyze a character by determining his character traits. To answer this critical question, you must go beyond the text and make a judgment about what you have read.

Look at the graphic organizer you just filled in. Choose the trait you think was most important in helping Jack and the one you think was least important. Write about each trait in a separate paragraph. Be sure to explain why you chose each trait. To help with your explanation, look at the event you listed for each trait.

4Rs   Remember to **Review**. When you are done, make sure that your writing is the best it can be by using the checklist on page 56.

DIRECTIONS: Read about a young man who learned to respect lions. Then you will use a Cause and Effect Map. It will help you explain why lions came to a certain village and how they affected the people there.

Living near Lions

by Cecil Dzwowa

In southern African countries—such as Zimbabwe, where I live—many people live close to wild animals. Different animals cause different problems for people.

Buffaloes, impalas, and other plant eaters can eat up people's food crops. But lions sometimes kill people and their livestock.

The village where I grew up, Chikombedzi, is close to the Gonarezhou National Park. This preserve is home to zebras and giraffes as well as antelopes such as wildebeests.

Wherever you find these animals, lions will always hang around. So there were also many lions in and around Gonarezhou. They sometimes left the park in search of food.

One day a man in my village—armed with only a spear—fought with a lion to protect his cattle. The lion left hungry, but the man was nearly killed.

Surprised by Lions

Lionesses and their cubs live in groups known as prides, and males live alone or together in small groups. So we knew we might see them in groups or alone.

But the thick grass and the bushes provided a good cover for the lions. Sometimes people would not be aware that a lion was nearby until it was already too close for them to get away.

People were so afraid of lions that they often walked in groups. In some remote villages, adults took turns escorting their children to school. In fact, my friends and I sometimes missed school because lions had been seen outside of the park.

One hot afternoon, my uncle, two of my friends, and I came frighteningly close to a wandering male lion. We were gathering wood to use as stakes to support tomato plants.

Just like the arrival of any other king, the lion's approach was signaled in style. Wild impalas and kudus usually stayed away from people. But suddenly several of them bolted into the village. Apparently they had smelled or heard the lion but did not know where it was. In their panic, they ran back and forth through the village before finally crashing away through the brush.

Baboons also signaled the lion's arrival. As usual, the baboons were hanging around the village, fighting among themselves and trying to steal food from villagers. Suddenly they scrambled up the trees. They climbed up and down again and again, screaming their warning calls.

Our two dogs, Isa and Bingo, tucked their tails between their legs and dared not move even an inch from us.

Brave Uncle Tendai

When the lion stepped out of the brush, the only person who stood his ground was my Uncle Tendai. He calmly helped my two friends and me to climb up a nearby tree. We were so frightened that our shivering shook the tree.

The lion was about thirty feet away, and I could see him clearly. He looked old, as the bottom part of his mane was turning whitish. He made an unconcerned gaze at our tree and at Uncle Tendai. The lion stood still for about a minute, and then leisurely moved away.

Lazy Lions

From the mountaintops, my friends and I sometimes saw lions lazily sleeping in the shade of baobab or msasa trees in the plains. They did not seem to care about us at all, and they would just carry on with their sleeping.

Lion attacks in the villages are actually rare. Only in times of serious drought do lions become a problem as they turn to the villages to attack livestock like cattle and goats.

In fact, people are a greater threat to lions than lions are to people. Some lions are shot by poachers, and lions everywhere are losing their habitat to humans.

Near my village, lions can be seen all over the plains. But the total number of wild lions in Africa is going down. They are listed as vulnerable to extinction, but not endangered.

Instead of trying to kill the lions, we villagers install scarecrows that hold gun-like sticks near the animal pens, which we call kraals. This helps frighten these giant cats.

Some people regard lions as sacred animals. Local belief says that some of the spirits of our grandparents live in certain lions. This belief has helped in saving lions not only from the villagers but from poachers, too.

Over time, I have tried to live peacefully side by side with Africa's famous meat eater. Sometimes these large carnivores seem to be greedy man-eating beasts. But in fact, they kill only for food. Lucky enough, people are not among their favorite choices.

For those of us who live close to them, lions are potentially dangerous neighbors. But if we respect them, we don't need to fear them.

Cause and Effect Map

A **Cause and Effect Map** helps you organize *causes* and *effects*. In this organizer, an event goes in the center box. To the left are boxes for the causes leading up to that event. This organizer has two boxes for causes, but you can have as many or as few as needed. To the right are boxes for the effects of the event. Once again, there are two boxes, but you can change the number to accommodate the passage.

Read the essay question and instructions on page 41.

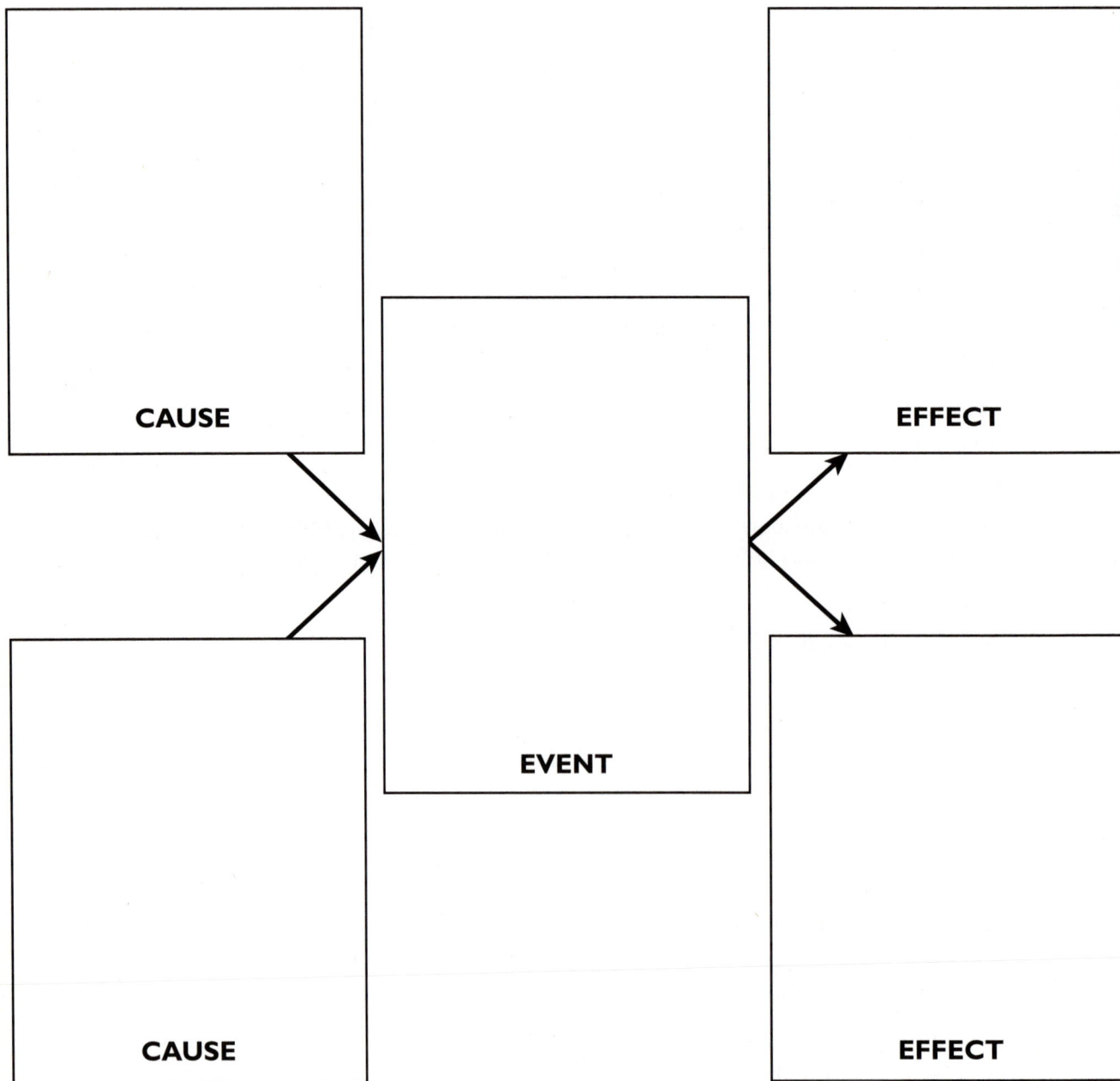

```
┌─────────────┐                    ┌─────────────┐
│             │                    │             │
│             │                    │             │
│   CAUSE     │─┐              ┌───│   EFFECT    │
│             │ └──►┌───────┐──┘   │             │
└─────────────┘     │       │      └─────────────┘
                    │       │
┌─────────────┐  ┌─►│       │──┐   ┌─────────────┐
│             │──┘  │ EVENT │  └──►│             │
│             │     └───────┘      │             │
│   CAUSE     │                    │   EFFECT    │
│             │                    │             │
└─────────────┘                    └─────────────┘
```

Essay Question: What brought the lions so close to the village, and how did this affect the lives of the people living there? Use details from the article to explain your answers.

1. To answer the question, you must know why the lions came to live so close to the village and what effect this had on the villagers. The event will be "Lions live close to people." Write this in the *event* box.

2. Go back to the article to find out how lions came to live so close to the village. Write the cause(s) in the boxes to the left of the event. Ignore a box if you find only one cause; add boxes if you find more than two causes.

3. Next, look at the article to see how the proximity of the lions affected the people living in the village. Write the effect(s) in the boxes to the right of the event box. Ignore one box if you find only one effect; add boxes if you find more than two effects.

Now that you have filled in the **Cause and Effect Map,** use it to answer the essay question at the top of the page. Write your answer on a separate sheet of paper.

Turn the Lock

This is a cause and effect question in which you must identify details from the article. To answer this interpretive question, you must put together different pieces of information from the passage to form your response.

Now use the graphic organizer to help you write your essay. Explain how the lions came to live so close to people. Then, describe the effects on the villagers.

4Rs Remember the fourth **R**. After you finish, use the checklist on page 56 to review your writing.

Speak Out

Suppose that you lived in Chikombedzi. Prepare a speech on the subject. Then give your speech to the class.

DIRECTIONS: The following poem is set during the Civil War. In 1862, Confederate troops, led by Generals Robert E. Lee and Stonewall Jackson, marched into the town of Frederick, Maryland. Although the people there were loyal to the Union, they were afraid to display the U.S. flag. Read this poem about the deed of a courageous woman. Then you will use an Event Map. It will help you describe what happens in the poem.

Barbara Frietchie

by John Greenleaf Whittier

Up from the meadows rich with corn,
Clear in the cool September morn,

The clustered spires of Frederick stand
Green-walled by the hills of Maryland.

Round about them orchards sweep,
Apple and peach tree fruited deep,

Fair as the garden of the Lord
To the eyes of the **famished** rebel horde,

On that pleasant morn of the early fall
When Lee marched over the mountain wall;

Over the mountains winding down
Horse and foot, into Frederick town.

Forty flags with their silver stars,
Forty flags with their crimson bars,

Flapped in the morning wind: the sun
Of noon looked down, and saw not one.

Up rose old Barbara Frietchie then,
Bowed with her **fourscore** years and ten;

Bravest of all in Frederick town,
She took up the flag the men hauled down;

In her attic window the staff she set,
To show that one heart was loyal yet.

Up the street came the rebel tread,
Stonewall Jackson riding ahead.

Under his slouched hat left and right
He glanced; the old flag met his sight.

"Halt!"—the dust-brown ranks stood fast.
"Fire!"—out blazed the rifle blast.

It shivered the window, pane and sash;
It rent the banner with seam and gash.

Quick, as it fell, from the broken staff
Dame Barbara snatched the silken scarf.

famished: very hungry, or starving
fourscore: four times twenty; eighty

She leaned far out on the windowsill,
And shook it forth with a royal will.

"Shoot, if you must, this old gray head,
But spare your country's flag," she said.

A shade of sadness, a blush of shame,
Over the face of the leader came;

The nobler nature within him stirred
To life at that woman's deed and word;

"Who touches a hair of yon gray head
Dies like a dog! March on!" he said.

All day long through Frederick street
Sounded the tread of marching feet:

All day long that free flag tossed
Over the heads of the rebel host.

Ever its torn folds rose and fell
On the loyal winds that loved it well;

And through the hill gaps sunset light
Shone over it with a warm good night.

Barbara Frietchie's work is o'er,
And the Rebel rides on his raids no more.

Honor to her! and let a tear
Fall, for her sake, on Stonewall's **bier.**

Over Barbara Frietchie's grave,
Flag of Freedom and Union, wave!

Peace and order and beauty draw
Round thy symbol of light and law;

And ever the stars above look down
On thy stars below in Frederick town!

bier: coffin and its supporting platform

Event Map

An **Event Map** helps you organize your thoughts by asking key questions, similar to those of a newspaper reporter. In this organizer, a question appears in each box. These questions ask the following: What? When? Where? Who? How? Why? Write each answer in the appropriate box.

Read the essay question and instructions on page 45.

What happened?

When did it happen?

Where did it happen?

Who was involved?

How did it happen?

Why did it happen?

Essay Question: Imagine that you are a reporter at the time of the Civil War. Write an informative article describing the events related in the poem.

1. The graphic organizer will help you gather the information you need to write your article. Look at the question in the first box. What was the main event that happened in the poem? Write it in the first box.

2. In the next two boxes write when and where the event happened.

3. In the third box, write the names of the characters involved. In the fourth box, give details on how the event unfolded.

4. In the last box, tell why the event happened. Why did Barbara Frietchie do what she did?

Now that you have filled in the **Event Map,** use it to answer the essay question at the top of the page. Write your answer on a separate sheet of paper.

Turn the Lock

This question asks you to summarize what you have read by identifying details from the poem. To answer this interpretive question, you must put together different pieces of information from the poem.

Look at the answers you wrote for each question on the graphic organizer. Think about how you would use these answers to write your article. Remember that you are writing the article from the viewpoint of a reporter during the Civil War. Think about how newspaper articles are organized. Try to mimic this organization when you write your article.

4Rs Remember to **Review.** Check your writing on page 56.

DIRECTIONS: Read the following article about an unusual ship. Then you will use a Main Idea Map. It will help you explain what this ship does.

Drilling in the Ocean Floor

by Jack Myers

If you were standing on this ship, you would see how odd-looking it is. It's called the *JOIDES Resolution*. Since 1985 it has been working its way through the oceans of the world. Most of that time it has stayed quietly at rest while it drilled holes in the ocean bottom. That's its job—to find out what's down there beneath the ocean floor.

The 147-foot-high **derrick** can haul up long sections of drill pipe. Then the sections are threaded together to make a continuous pipe that can be lowered all the way to the ocean bottom.

There are a lot of sharp teeth at the end of the pipe. That makes it work like a long, skinny cookie cutter. As the pipe is turned round and round and pushed downward, a pencil-shaped cookie of sediment and rock is pushed upward inside the pipe. It is called a core.

Special tools will pull a 30-foot-long piece of core up to the ship. Then there will be a cry of "Core on deck!"—and all hands will rush to the drilling deck. Carefully they will carry the core to the ship's laboratory, where it will be studied and then labeled and stored.

Altogether, the ship has collected a total of more than a hundred miles of cores. They make up a library of the seafloor's sediment and rocks for scientists to study.

JOIDES Resolution had made a whole series of discoveries. Some tell about what happened in ages past, others tell about what is happening today.

An Energy Source?

One discovery has taught us more about a mysterious chemical called a gas hydrate. It occurs as ice-like deposits of methane and water deep beneath the ocean floor. (Methane is the stuff we call natural gas.)

derrick: a beam with rope used to lift and move heavy objects

Gas hydrate is hard to study because it decomposes when taken from the high pressures at which it was formed. It took an invention of a pressure core sampler to bring samples up to the ship for study. The surprise was in how much of the stuff was found. Scientists of the program believe that the total amount of gas hydrate down there is greater than all other kinds of fossil fuel (coal, oil, and gas) put together. Someday in the future we may find a way to recover it.

Heat from Below

I think the most exciting discoveries are in what's happening right now beneath the seafloor. Far below, around the earth's center, there is a hot, hot liquid iron core. Its heat slowly rises through a thick layer called the mantle and up to the crust below the ocean floor.

We think of the mantle as being mostly rock, but it slowly flows under high temperature and pressure. So in a sluggish way the mantle behaves as a layer of thick liquid heated from below. The hottest places expand, become less dense, and rise. Since mantle composition is not the same all over, some places are better at carrying heat upward. They cause hot spots in the crust above.

A hot spot in the crust under the ocean floor gives lots of action. The crust is made of rocks with cracks and crevices between them. That creates channels where cold seawater can trickle down into hot places and other channels where the heated seawater is rising.

So hot seawater is continuously trickling, or percolating, through channels in the rock. Percolation is a process often used by chemists to extract materials that can dissolve in water. (In kitchens it is used by some coffee makers to extract coffee from crushed coffee beans.)

Because it's under great pressure, the super hot seawater can't boil, but it's great at dissolving stuff out of the rock. Some of the stuff "undissolves" again when it reaches the cold water above. That leaves big deposits of minerals extracted from the crust.

The idea of seafloor percolation is not a new one, but *JOIDES Resolution* has learned how it works. Instruments were left in several boreholes, and their information was retrieved several years later. That information confirmed the percolator idea and showed how big a percolating system can be—in one case a mile wide and more than a mile deep.

These percolators churn up the seafloor. They deposit sulfur-containing minerals that provide food for seafloor bacteria. Those bacteria are food for animals that have never been seen up where we live. And studying how the percolators work tells us a lot about how our mineral deposits were formed in ages past. The *JOIDES Resolution* is letting us look at parts of the earth we never saw before.

Main Idea Map

A **Main Idea Map** helps you organize a selection's main idea, or the most important idea in the selection. In this organizer, the main idea goes in the center circle. Attached to the circle are lines for *subtopics*. This organizer has four lines for subtopics attached to the circle, but you can have as many or as few as you need. Attached to each subtopic line are three lines for *details* about the subtopic. Again, you can adjust the number of detail lines to fit the passage.

Read the essay question and instructions on page 49.

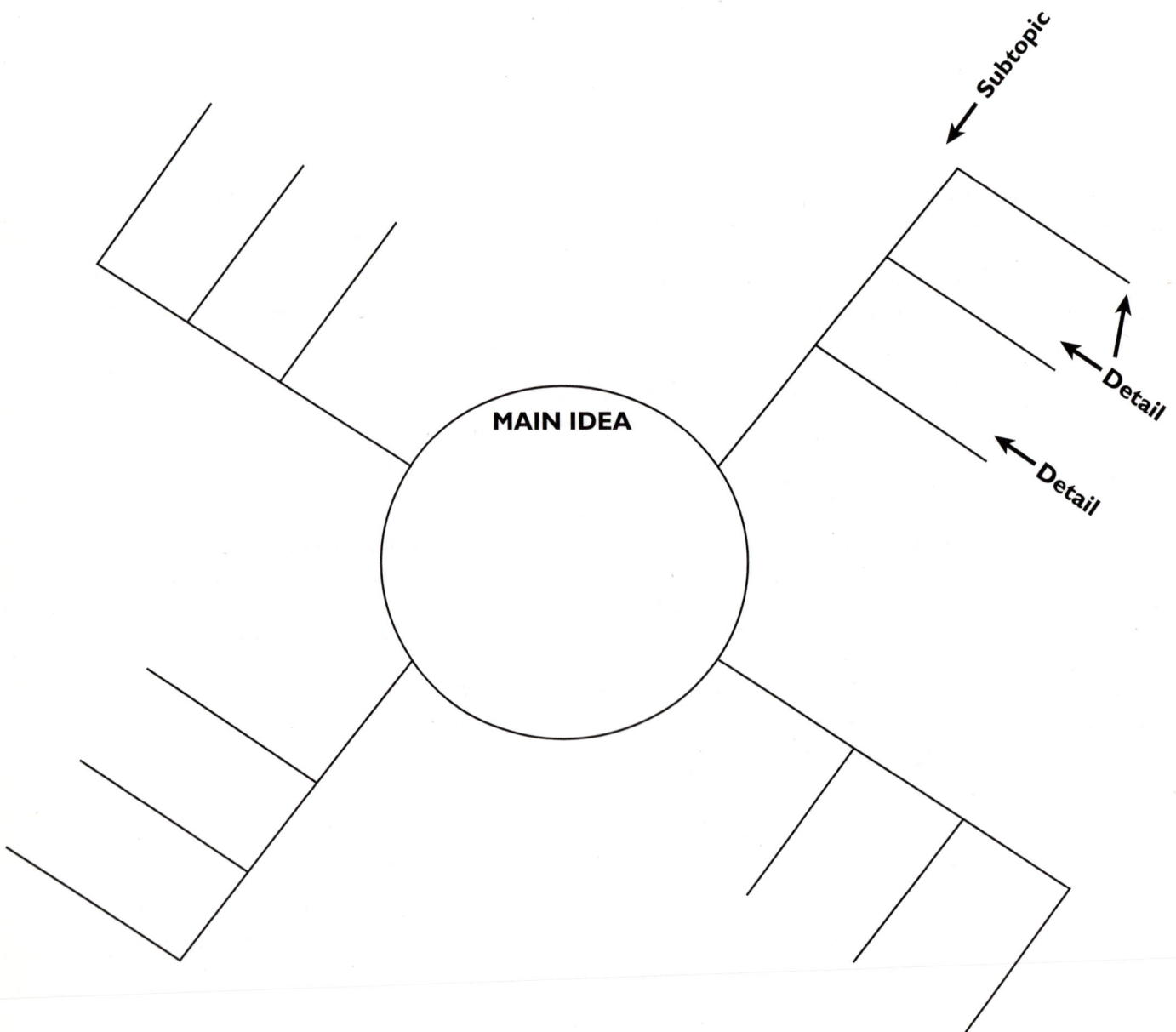

MAIN IDEA

Subtopic

Detail

Detail

This page may not be reproduced without permission of Steck-Vaughn/Berrent.

Essay Question: How does the *JOIDES Resolution* let us look at parts of the earth we never saw before? Use details and examples from the article.

1. First, think about the main idea of the article. The article tells you about *JOIDES Resolution*, but what does it tell you? What is the job of the ship? The answer to this question will give you the main idea. Write the main idea in the center circle.

2. Next, you have to find the subtopics. The article tells you how the *JOIDES Resolution* does its work. It also relates two important discoveries—finding information about gas hydrate and discovering how percolation works beneath the sea. These are three separate subtopics. Write them on three of the subtopic lines. You will not be using the fourth line for this passage.

3. Now look for details on each subtopic. These go in the lines attached to each subtopic line. You can add more lines if you need to do so.

Now that you have filled in the **Main Idea Map,** use it to answer the essay question at the top of the page. Write your answer on a separate sheet of paper.

Turn the Lock

This question asks you to discuss the main idea of the article by using supporting details. To answer this interpretive question, you must put together different pieces of information from the passage.

Use the information on your Main Idea Map to answer the essay question. To describe how the *JOIDES Resolution* shows us parts of the earth we never saw before, explain how the ship does its job and give detailed examples of its two important discoveries.

4Rs   Remember to **Review.** Use the checklist on page 56 to review your work.

DIRECTIONS: Read the following story about a fateful reunion. Then you will use a Story Map. It will help you describe the story and its effect on you.

After Twenty Years

by O. Henry

The policeman on the beat moved up the avenue impressively. The impressiveness was habitual and not for show, for spectators were few. The time was barely ten o'clock at night, but chilly gusts of wind with a taste of rain in them had **well nigh** depeopled the streets.

Trying doors as he went, twirling his club with many intricate and artful movements, turning now and then to cast his watchful eye down the **pacific thoroughfare,** the officer, with his stalwart form and slight swagger, made a fine picture of a guardian of the peace. The vicinity was one that kept early hours. Now and then you might see the lights of a cigar store or of an all-night lunch counter; but the majority of the doors belonged to business places that had long since been closed.

When about midway of a certain block, the policeman suddenly slowed his walk. In the doorway of a darkened hardware store a man leaned, with an unlighted cigar in his mouth. As the policeman walked up to him, the man spoke up quickly.

"It's all right, officer," he said, reassuringly. "I'm just waiting for a friend. It's an appointment made twenty years ago. Sounds a little funny to you, doesn't it? Well, I'll explain if you'd like to make certain it's all straight. About that long ago there used to be a restaurant where this store stands—'Big Joe' Brady's restaurant."

well nigh: almost
pacific thoroughfare: quiet street

"Until five years ago," said the policeman. "It was torn down then."

The man in the doorway struck a match and lit his cigar. The light showed a pale, square-jawed face with keen eyes, and a little white scar near his right eyebrow. His scarfpin was a large diamond, oddly set.

"Twenty years ago tonight," said the man. "I dined here at 'Big Joe' Brady's with Jimmy Wells, my best chum, and the finest chap in the world. He and I were raised here in New York, just like two brothers, together. I was eighteen and Jimmy was twenty. The next morning I was to start for the West to make my fortune. You couldn't have dragged Jimmy out of New York, he thought it was the only place on earth. Well, we agreed that night that we would meet here again exactly twenty years from that date and time, no matter what our conditions might be or from what distance we might have to come. We figured that in twenty years each of us ought to have our destiny worked out and our fortunes made, whatever they were going to be."

"It sounds pretty interesting," said the policeman. "Rather a long time between meets, though, it seems to me. Haven't you heard from your friend since you left?"

"Well, yes, for a time we corresponded," said the other. "But after a year or two we lost track of each other. You see, the West is a pretty big proposition, and I kept hustling around over it pretty lively. But I know Jimmy will meet me here if he's still alive, for he always was the truest, staunchest old chap in the world. He'll never forget. I came a thousand miles to stand in this door tonight, and it's worth it if my old partner turns up."

The waiting man pulled out a handsome watch, the lids of it set with small diamonds.

"Three minutes to ten," he announced. "It was exactly ten o'clock when we parted here at the restaurant door."

"Did pretty well out West, didn't you?" asked the policeman.

"You bet! I hope Jimmy has done half as well. He was a kind of plodder, though, good fellow as he was. I've had to compete with some of the sharpest wits going to get my pile. A man gets in a groove in New York. It takes the West to put a razor-edge on him."

The policeman twirled his club and took a step or two.

"I'll be on my way. Hope your friend comes around all right. Going to call time on him sharp?"

"I should say not!" said the other. "I'll give him half an hour at least. If Jimmy is alive on earth he'll be here by that time. So long, Officer."

"Good-night, sir," said the policeman, passing on along his beat, trying doors as he went.

There was now a fine, cold drizzle falling, and the wind had risen from its uncertain puffs into a steady blow. The few foot passengers astir in that quarter hurried dismally and silently along with coat collars turned high and pocketed hands. And in the door of the hardware store the man who had come a thousand miles to fill an appointment, uncertain almost to absurdity, with the friend of his youth, smoked his cigar and waited.

About twenty minutes he waited, and then a tall man in a long overcoat, with collar turned up to his ears, hurried across from the opposite side of the street. He went directly to the waiting man.

"Is that you, Bob?" he asked doubtfully.

"Is that you, Jimmy Wells?" cried the man in the door.

"Bless my heart!" exclaimed the new arrival, grasping both the other's hands with his own. "It's Bob, sure as fate. I was certain I'd find you here if you were still in existence. Well, well, well!—twenty years is a long time. The old restaurant's gone, Bob; I wish it had lasted, so we could have had another dinner there. How has the West treated you, old man?"

"**Bully**; it has given me everything I asked it for. You've changed lots, Jimmy. I never thought you were so tall by two or three inches."

"Oh, I grew a bit after I was twenty."

"Doing well in New York, Jimmy?"

"Moderately. I have a position in one of the city's departments. Come on, Bob; we'll go around to a place I know of, and have a good long talk about old times."

The two men started up the street, arm in arm. The man from the West, his egotism

bully: very well

enlarged by success, was beginning to outline the history of his career. The other, submerged in his overcoat, listened with interest.

At the corned stood a drugstore, brilliant with electric lights. When they came into this glare each of them turned simultaneously to gaze upon the other's face.

The man from the West stopped suddenly and released his arm.

"You're not Jimmy Wells," he snapped. "Twenty years is a long time, but not long enough to change a man's nose from a Roman to a pug."

"It sometimes changes a good man into a bad one," said the tall man. "You've been under arrest for ten minutes, 'Silky' Bob. Chicago thinks you may have dropped over our way and wires us she wants to have a chat with you. Going quietly, are you? That's sensible. Now, before we go to the station here's a note I was asked to hand to you. You may read it here at the window. It's from Patrolman Wells."

The man from the West unfolded the little piece of paper handed him. His hand was steady when he began to read, but it trembled a little by the time he had finished. The note was rather short.

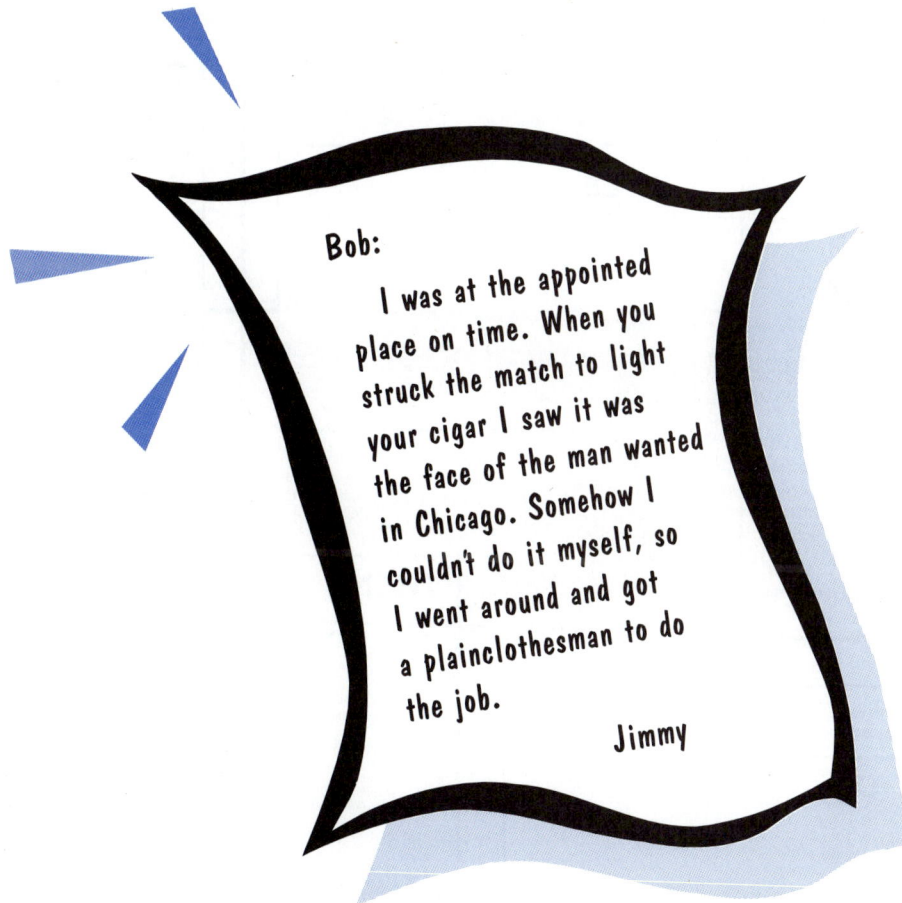

> Bob:
>
> I was at the appointed place on time. When you struck the match to light your cigar I saw it was the face of the man wanted in Chicago. Somehow I couldn't do it myself, so I went around and got a plainclothesman to do the job.
>
> Jimmy

Story Map

A **Story Map** helps you understand the parts of a story and see how they are related. In this organizer, you write the title of the story in the center box. Then you fill in each of the other boxes with the appropriate information from the story.

Read the essay question and instructions on page 55.

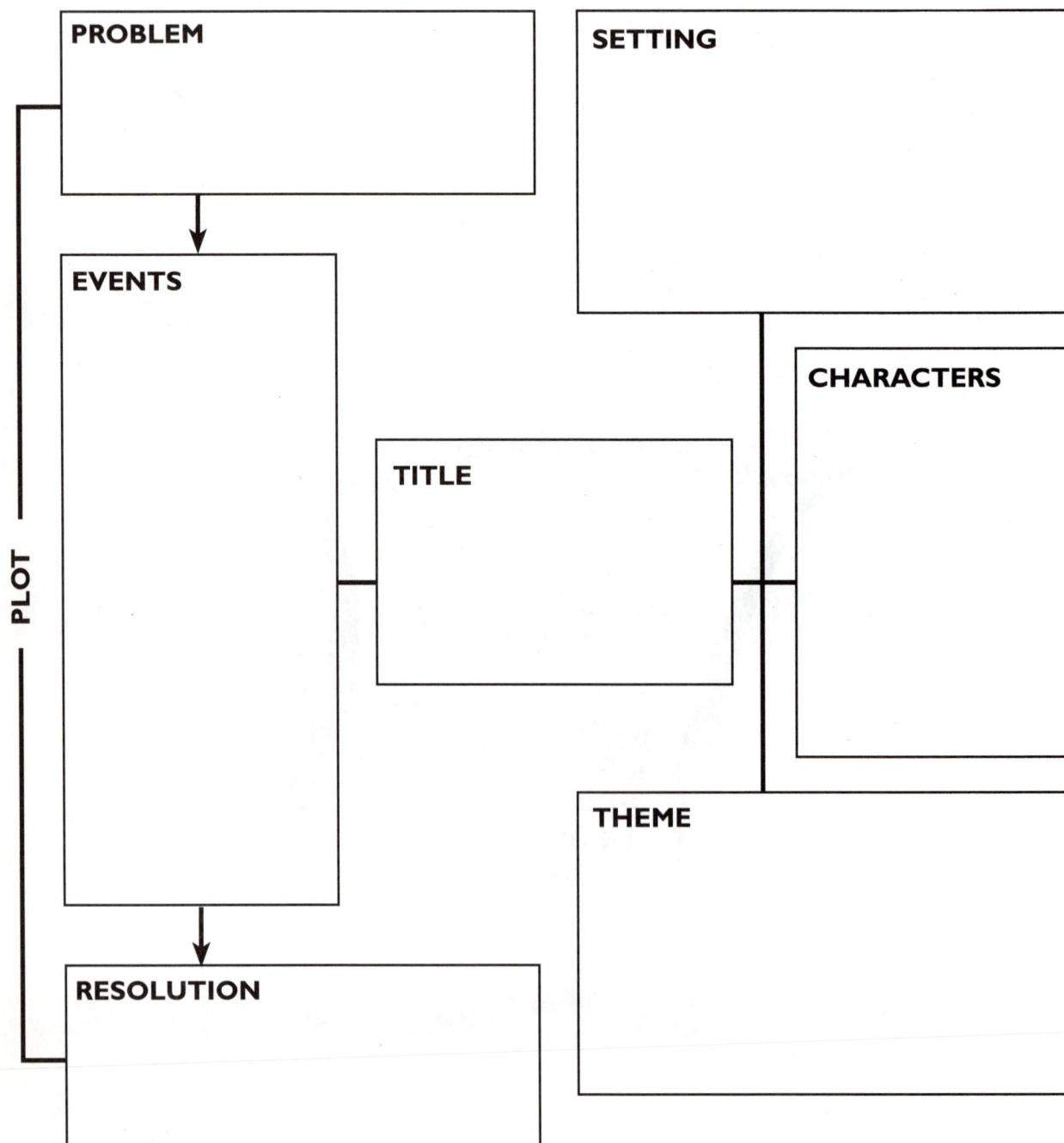

PROBLEM

SETTING

EVENTS

PLOT

TITLE

CHARACTERS

THEME

RESOLUTION

Essay Question: What impression does the story make on you? Describe how the plot, characters, setting, and theme of the story all contribute to this effect.

1. Write the title of the story in the center box. Then look at the boxes to the left. What is the main problem in the story? What situation must patrolman Wells solve? Write the problem in the top box on the left. Then, in the box below, write the main events from the story. In the last box in the row, tell how the problem is resolved.

2. Now look at the boxes to the right of the title. Where and when does the story take place? Write your answer in the setting box. In the box below, list the characters from the story. The last box is for the theme. What idea does the story relay about life and the way people can change? Write your answer in the theme box.

Now that you have filled in the **Story Map,** use it to answer the essay question at the top of the page. Write your answer on a separate sheet of paper.

Open the Door

This question asks you to evaluate and extend meaning by identifying details from the story. To answer this critical question, you must make a judgment about what you have read.

Look at the graphic organizer you just filled in. Then think about what effect the story has on you. How does it make you feel? How do the elements of the story listed in the Story Map contribute to this effect?

4Rs   Remember to **Review.** Use the checklist on page 56 to review your work.

✔ After You Write

Use this list to check your writing.

Revise:
- ☐ Did you meet the purpose of the task?
- ☐ Did you stay on the topic?
- ☐ Is there an opening and a closing?
- ☐ Did you support your main ideas with details?
- ☐ Did you organize your ideas clearly?
- ☐ Did you vary your words and sentences?

- ☐ Do all the words make sense?
- ☐ Is your writing interesting?
- ☐ Is your writing easy to read?

Edit:
- ☐ Do verbs agree with their subjects?
- ☐ Are pronouns used correctly?
- ☐ Are the spelling, capitalization, and punctuation correct?

Summary

In this unit, you learned that you can use graphic organizers to help you recall and understand what you have read. Graphic organizers can also help you answer essay questions about a passage by allowing you to collect ideas and categorize them before you begin to write.

You have learned about the following graphic organizers:

 **Compare-Contrast Grid**

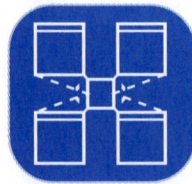 **Character Traits Map**

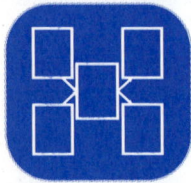 **Cause and Effect Map**

 **Event Map**

 **Main Idea Map**

 **Story Map**

 Remember that when answering an essay question, you should always use the **Four *Rs*: R**eady, **R**ead, **R**espond, **R**eview. When you review your work, use a checklist such as the one above.

Guided Practice

Now you are going to practice what you have learned by reading several selections and answering multiple-choice, short-answer, and essay questions about them. These questions will be at the three key levels of comprehension: literal, interpretive, and critical. You will be given a hint to help you answer each question.

Regardless of what type of selection you read or question you answer, you should always follow the **Four _R_s:**

4Rs

Ready—Get ready to read

Read—Read the selection

Respond—Answer the question

Review—Check your answer

DIRECTIONS: Read this article about a very wet celebration. Then answer questions 1 through 6. Darken the circle at the bottom of the page or write your answer on the lines.

Thingyan: New Year in Myanmar

by Marci Stillerman

So So throws a bucket of cool water at her brother, Mo Mo, soaking him to the skin. So So is already soaked, but she screams with delight when Mo Mo throws a pail of water at her.

Up and down the streets of Yangon, people are throwing water at one another. Hoses and pumps are turned on. Everyone is wet. The buildings and temples are dripping. The streets are awash with water and soon begin to look like tiny rivers. The air is oven-hot, and the wet streets steam. But the drenched people feel wonderfully cool.

"Be soaked in cool water. Happy New Year!" they call to one another. "May the new year be as comforting as this water!"

It is April in Yangon, the capital city of Myanmar (formerly Burma), a country in Southeast Asia on the Bay of Bengal. It is the hottest and driest month of the year; even the major rivers have become mere trickles of water. In some areas of Myanmar, water and food are scarce. People hope that the rainy season will start soon to cool the land and provide moisture so crops can be planted. When the monsoon storms do begin, rain will pour from the skies so heavily that a man out in the field won't be able to see his oxcart in front of him.

It is the season of Thingyan, the celebration of the new year. Thingyan usually falls around the middle of April. The actual date is decided by Hindu astrologers, and the festival carries on for three to four days. Thingyan is the biggest and most important celebration in the annual cycle of festivals in Myanmar. It is celebrated in the hope that the rains will come on time.

Thingyan means water festival to the Burmese and is associated with the Buddhist god Thagyamin. (Buddhism is the major religion of Myanmar.) During the three to four days of celebration, Buddhists believe that Thagyamin descends to earth to bring blessings for the new year. Carrying a conch shell, he rides a variety of mythical mounts—serpent, lion, or winged golden horse—which are interpreted by the astrologers to determine what kind of year it will be—wet, dry, *prosperous*, or poor. At the end of the new-year festival, Thagyamin returns to his seat in the heavens.

The people of Myanmar know how important water is to their lives. Water means survival. Not only must they have water for drinking, washing, and cooking, but water is also needed to grow rice, their most important food. In order to grow, rice seedlings are planted in paddies flooded with water.

The people of Myanmar have always regarded water as precious. Jars of water are present in all religious ceremonies, and a gift of water brings blessings. They also share their precious water with strangers. In the country's remotest villages, travelers find a *ye oh sin* (yeah ooh sin), or water jar with dipper attached. It may sit in its own little house on stilts by the walkway or entrance to a house. The terra-cotta jar is porous so that small amounts of water evaporate on the outside, cooling the water inside. Small green shoots are planted in the sand nearby to lighten the hearts of the weary. A Burmese prayer expresses the spirit behind the offering of water:

May he be cool as water and fresh as flowers.

Early in the morning during Thingyan, drummers beat their drums as they call people to follow them down the streets of Yangon on their way to the temples to wash Buddhist images. Young and old alike are full of excitement as they pour out of their houses to follow the drummers.

Tremendous floats adorned with fruits and flowers—offerings for the temples—also come down the streets, which are decorated with small flags, flowers, colored paper streamers, and children's drawings. People riding on the floats splash buckets of water on the passersby. Children and adults pour water from bottles and pails all over one another. Drenching a friend is a sign of affection and good wishes. Buddhists believe that water washes away evil deeds and helps people begin the new year clean and pure.

People then return to their homes, where younger family members pay their respects to their elders and ask forgiveness for any wrongdoings. There is much feasting and visiting among relatives and friends during these days. Most of all, everyone looks forward to eating the special foods that have been prepared just for this festival.

In other parts of Myanmar, such as the city of Mandalay or the state of Rakhine, Thingyan is also celebrated with dancing and contests. At night, processions of beautifully decorated floats alight with torches fill the streets.

By the last day of Thingyan the paved streets and buildings of Yangon are sparkling clean. People go to the temples to pray for health and happiness in the new year and to make donations to the temple or monastery. They also pray for peace throughout the world.

1 In Myanmar, the month in which Thingyan is celebrated is the—

A coldest and wettest month of the year

B hottest and driest month of the year

C hottest and wettest month of the year

D coldest and driest month of the year

Hint Identify details from the article. In what month does Thingyan take place? What does the article tell you about the weather during this month?

2 What does the word *prosperous* mean in the article?

F sorrowful

G fleeting

H favorable

J scanty

Hint This is a vocabulary question. Read the sentence in the article that contains prosperous. Which of these words would make the most sense in the sentence.

3 The *best* way to find out more about Thingyan is to—

A visit an Asian museum

B look up *Thingyan* in a dictionary

C look in an encyclopedia under "new year celebrations"

D read a book about Buddhist celebrations in Myanmar

Hint Determine characteristics of informational texts. Think about which source would provide the most information about the topic.

Answers

1 Ⓐ Ⓑ Ⓒ Ⓓ	2 Ⓕ Ⓖ Ⓗ Ⓙ	3 Ⓐ Ⓑ Ⓒ Ⓓ

4 Why is water so important to the people of Myanmar?

_____

_____

_____

_____

_____

_____

Hint Identify details from the article. Look for key words in the selection that are similar to those in the question to help you find this information.

5 How reliable do you think the information in this article is? Explain your response.

_____

_____

_____

_____

_____

_____

Hint Understand the reliability of the author. Think about what makes a source dependable. Does this article fit those qualifications?

6 Imagine that you are attending your first Thingyan in Myanmar. Write about your impressions of the celebration. What do you find most unusual? What is most impressive? What, if anything, do you dislike? What do you think you have gained by attending the celebration?

Use a graphic organizer to plan your essay.

Draw a Main Idea Map to help you organize your thoughts about Thingyan. Your main idea should state in general terms what Thingyan is. The subtopics should cover how it is celebrated, why it is celebrated, and what occurs during the celebration. Then fill in the details about each subtopic.

Write your essay on the lines below. If you need more space, continue writing on a separate sheet of paper.

_____

_____

_____

_____

_____

_____

_____

_____

_____

_____

_____

_____

_____

Hint Extend meaning of the passage by determining the main idea. Think about how you would feel if you attended Thingyan. Look at all the questions that you must answer in your essay. Use the information on the Main Idea Map to help you answer them. After you finish, use the checklist on page 56 to help you review your writing.

DIRECTIONS: **Read this story about a family who has some close encounters with raccoons. Then answer questions 7 through 12. Darken the circle at the bottom of the page or write your answer on the lines.**

Raccoon Summer

by Mary L. Johnson

People aren't the only ones who enjoy fast food and takeout.

Our family has always liked birds, so we keep feeders, houses, and birdbaths available all year. Birds can enjoy a fast-food meal of sunflower seeds or mixed seeds whenever they like. For the takeout crowd, unshelled peanuts make a great grab-and-go treat.

One particularly dry summer, when wild grasses and berries were scarce near our home in southern New Jersey, we noticed new visitors at our ground-level feeders. Groundhogs were raiding the bowls of sunflower seeds during the day, and raccoons and opossums were snacking on them at night.

As the drought worsened, we began to place stale and leftover foods outside for these animals. While opossums enjoyed dry cat food and raisins, raccoons seemed to have a sweet tooth. When offered the choice of carrots, seeds, apples, or frosted, fruit-flavored cereal rings, the raccoons chose the cereal rings every time. They also enjoyed cookies, stale doughnuts, and cupcakes, which they would hold comically in their front paws while nibbling.

It didn't take the raccoons long to figure out that all their favorite goodies were brought to them through a set of sliding glass doors opening onto our back deck. Any night that goodies failed to appear, these clever raccoons would scamper right up to the doors and bang on the glass with their front paws until someone appeared to wait on them. "Service, please!" they seemed to say.

One evening we put out a large roasting pan with the scanty remains of a turkey inside. We watched as two raccoons worked together to drag their takeout dinner through a break in the backyard fence, pan and all. About a week later, the same raccoons reappeared, dragging the now-empty pan back with them. They left it upside down at the end of the backyard. Were they hoping for a free refill, maybe?

These two raccoons took advantage of our personalized service regularly throughout the summer, eventually bringing three babies along with them. The male would always stand guard while the rest of his family ate. He was stuck with leftovers whenever they were finished.

On the night before garbage collection, when all the trash cans in the neighborhood were waiting at the curb, the raccoons would tear open garbage bags and have a **smorgasbord.** One of the baby raccoons appeared on our back deck one evening with the remains of a large glass jar around its neck. Apparently, the raccoon had stuck its head inside the jar for a meal, then became trapped. Somehow, it had managed to break most of the jar away, but the rim and sharp splinters of glass remained around the raccoon's neck like a deadly collar. The young raccoon was growing quickly, and as the days passed, the jar rim became tighter and tighter. If it were not removed, the poor raccoon would be slowly strangled to death.

Could we use what we'd learned about raccoons that summer to help save it? My sister and I concocted a plan. First, we would lure the raccoon as close to the house as possible. Then, using a straightened coat hanger, we would try to hook the glass rim that was around the raccoon's neck and pull it off.

We waited. When we didn't see the baby raccoon for over a week, we felt terrible. What if we were too late? But, finally, the raccoon reappeared on the tenth day. My sister lured it right up to the sliding glass doors with old favorites such as frosted-fruit cereal and sugar cookies. The glass rim was visibly tighter now, squeezing the raccoon's small neck like a noose. We would have to work fast.

I eased the coat hanger through a crack in the sliding doors and carefully hooked it around the rim as the raccoon feasted. I leaned back and pulled, but nothing happened. The raccoon was startled and tried to back away. A tug of war started, with the raccoon pulling one way and me pulling the other.

The glass rim finally shattered from the pressure. I fell over backward holding the coat hanger, and the poor raccoon rolled right off the edge of the deck. It was so surprised, it ran up the nearest tree and stayed there for hours. My sister and I gathered up the glass shards and threw them away. The raccoon was saved!

It was back again the following night, as if nothing had happened. There was a bloody dent all around its neck, where the rim had been. The wound healed over the course of the summer, but a circular scar, like a necklace, always remained.

As the drought eased, the other raccoons returned to the wild foods that they were used to. But the raccoon we had nicknamed "Necklace" came regularly to our back deck until well into the winter, banging on the sliding glass doors for service.

The following summer, the same raccoon returned, still noticeably scarred, bringing three babies of her own along with her. Wild food was plentiful that year, so she didn't show up every day. But once a week or so, she would bring the kids to our back deck for the raccoon version of a fast-food treat.

smorgasbord: a Swedish word for a meal with a wide variety of dishes

7 The boxes show some events that happen in the story.

Two raccoons drag turkey leftovers in a pan through the fence.		The two raccoons bring three babies with them.
1	2	3

Which event belongs in Box 2?

F   The raccoons begin to bang on the glass doors for food.

G   The raccoons leave the upside-down pan in the backyard.

H   The family puts out seeds for birds.

J   A baby raccoon appears with a jar around its neck.

Hint   What is the order of events in the story? Find each event in the story. In what order did the events happen?

8 Which word *best* describes the narrator and her sister?

A humane   **C** comical

B selfish   **D** idle

Hint   Determine character traits. Think about what the two girls do in the story. How would you describe the girls' actions?

9 Which of the following *best* represents the author's viewpoint?

F   People should protect animals.

G   Animals can be a nuisance.

H   Feeding wild animals can cause problems.

J   Children should have pets.

Hint   Understand the author's point of view. Which statement best agrees with the events in the story?

Answers

7 Ⓕ Ⓖ Ⓗ Ⓙ	8 Ⓐ Ⓑ Ⓒ Ⓓ	9 Ⓕ Ⓖ Ⓗ Ⓙ

10 Why is the baby raccoon in danger from the glass jar around its neck?

_____

_____

_____

_____

_____

Hint Identify details in the story. Go back and read the section of the story where the baby with the glass jar first shows up.

11 What do you think is the author's purpose in writing this story?

_____

_____

_____

_____

_____

Hint Infer the author's purpose. Remember that the basic purposes for writing are to inform or explain, persuade, entertain, or describe.

12 The second half of the story tells how the narrator and her sister free a baby raccoon whose neck is caught by a glass jar. Explain the significance of this event in revealing character and theme.

Use a graphic organizer to plan your essay.

Before you can answer this, you should recall as much as you can about the event. Draw an Event Map for the incident when the girls free the baby raccoon.

Write your essay on the lines below. If you need more space, continue writing on a separate sheet of paper.

_____

_____

_____

_____

_____

_____

_____

_____

_____

_____

_____

_____

_____

_____

_____

Hint Determine theme and character traits. Look at the answers you wrote on the Event Map. What do you think is the significance of this event? What does it tell you about the two girls? How does it contribute to the theme or central message? After you finish your essay, remember to use the checklist on page 56 to help you review your writing.

DIRECTIONS: **Read this article to find out what life was like in the year 1001. Then answer questions 13 through 18. Darken the circle at the bottom of the page or write your answer on the lines.**

Blast to the Past

by Michael N. Smith

Let's say you're 12 years old. You wake up at daybreak to a rooster's crow, jump into your woolen sack tunic and leggings, and grab a quick breakfast of donkey milk. Stepping outside, you help your father harness the oxen to furrow the earth on your family farm with an iron wheel.

Leading the oxen, you and dad plow, and plow, and plow some more until your mom calls you both in for a dinner of vegetable gruel and hard bread.

Such was the life of an ordinary 12-year-old living in Western Europe in the year 1001.

Toilet Holes and Moss T.P.

In the year 1001, the average kid's house was located on a small plot of land often owned by a wealthy lord. The floor was covered with straw that was crawling with insects. In the summer, the rank odor of sheep, cow, and horse dung dominated the home. It didn't help that farm animals such as pigs lived inside the house!

The bathroom was the pits—literally. It was a hole dug outside near the back of the house, and moss, grass, and leaves were used as toilet paper. No one actually took a bath there. Streams and ponds served as bathtubs during warm weather. During winter, water for bathing was heated over the fire.

Do You Drool for Gruel?

Kids often dined on hard bread baked the week earlier and vegetable porridge, a soupy, oatmeal-like concoction. Forks weren't popular for another 600 years, so everyone chowed down with their hands.

Chicken and beef were luxuries, so kids ate pickled pork. On special occasions, mom would make a tasty sausage treat. Its main ingredient: pig's blood.

But lucky medieval kids didn't have to eat spinach, broccoli, and brussels sprouts. Those veggies wouldn't appear in Europe for several hundred years. On the menu instead were peas, beans, and cabbage.

Let's Toss Around the Old Pig Bladder

Sports-minded peasant boys played their own version of football with an inflated pig bladder. Girls engaged in footraces.

The medieval versions of TV, CDs, and Internet entertainment were storytelling and singing. Adults told kids tales of heroic warriors slaying dragons to protect villagers.

If You Can Read This, You're Too Modern

Kids didn't go to school, so most people never learned to read or write. Instead, they memorized and recited long, complicated folk poems taught by their elders.

Though poems taught kids about history and culture, other bits of information may have been better left *untaught*, like the idea that infection was caused by evil spirits firing invisible darts at the body. Of course, you couldn't blame the adults—with little scientific knowledge, medieval folks explained things the only way they knew how.

Home Shopping Network

Shopping malls? They're a distant dream. So mom made woolen tunics for kids to wear all year long.

Medieval villagers may not have had much by today's standards, but most people didn't think about stealing. There were no prisons, so wealthy thieves and murderers could pay a fine to get out of trouble. The alternative for the rest? Whipping, branding, head–shaving, or hanging to death.

Touch a Dead Man's Tooth and Call Me in the Morning

Almost all families lived in villages, often near dense forests full of firewood and berries. And though wild animals and outlaws lurked in the forest, the villagers hid there from pillaging Vikings. Without a police force, villagers were on their own.

Villagers were also without doctors and dentists, but they didn't worry too much. For a toothache, they could be "cured" by touching the tooth of a dead man. (If it didn't work, the live person's tooth could always be pulled.) And using the boiled-down fat of a recently dead criminal would cure just about any ailment.

Hitched by 14, History by 40

By her early teens, a girl from the noble class was married, often to a much older man.

A peasant girl didn't get hitched until she was older. But if she were still single by her mid-20s, she could always become a spinning wheel operator. (Guess where the word *"spinster"* comes from!) Then she'd have time for a nice long career—if she were lucky enough to live to 40!

Yep, life was short back in the year 1001. But who says it wasn't sweet, as well? After all, a strong sense of family and hardly any crime are things we could all use a little more of.

And of course, no school or spinach would be nice, too!

13 The word *spinster* comes from—

 A a medieval game played by girls

 B a garment worn by single women

 C a female spinning wheel operator

 D a long, complicated folk poem

> **Hint** Identify details in the article. Look for key words in the question that will lead you to the answer in the selection.

14 The tone of this article can *best* be described as—

 F informal

 G ironic

 H serious

 J passionate

> **Hint** Tone is the writer's attitude toward his or her audience and subject.

15 Which of these is an *opinion* from the article?

 A There were no prisons, so wealthy thieves and murderers could pay a fine to get out of trouble.

 B After all, a strong sense of family and hardly any crime are things we could all use a little more of.

 C Kids didn't go to school, so most people never learned to read or write.

 D Forks weren't popular for another 600 years, so everyone chowed down with their hands.

> **Hint** An opinion is what someone believes to be true. It cannot be proven.

Answers

13 Ⓐ Ⓑ Ⓒ Ⓓ	14 Ⓕ Ⓖ Ⓗ Ⓙ	15 Ⓐ Ⓑ Ⓒ Ⓓ

16 Why did people only live to about 40 years old in 1001? Use details from the
article to support your answer.

_____

_____

_____

_____

_____

_____

Hint Draw a conclusion based on the text. Reread part of the selection
that might give you clues as to reasons why people died young in
medieval times.

17 Why would this article not be appropriate for an encyclopedia?

_____

_____

_____

_____

_____

_____

Hint Determine characteristics of informational texts. Think about the
differences in structure and purpose between a magazine article and
an encyclopedia article.

18 Compare and contrast your life with that of a teenager in Western Europe in the year 1001.

Use a graphic organizer to plan your essay.

Draw a Compare-Contrast Grid to organize your thoughts about how life in the year 1001 is like your present life and how it is different. Write about things such as hygiene, food, sports and games, education, crime, and/or health.

Write your essay on the lines below. If you need more space, continue writing on a separate sheet of paper.

_____

_____

_____

_____

_____

_____

_____

_____

_____

_____

_____

_____

Hint Extend the meaning of the passage by comparing and contrasting information from the selection with life as you know it today. Use the information on the Compare-Contrast Grid to write your essay. Since you probably will not be able to write about everything you listed, narrow down the points you want to make. Start your essay by telling how your life is similar to that of a teenager in 1001. Then tell how your life is different. After you finish, use the checklist on page 56 to help you review your writing.

Speak Out

Suppose you could go back in time and live in 1001. What would you like most about living in that time period? What would you find the most difficult? Prepare a speech explaining your feelings about living in 1001. Then give your speech to the class.

DIRECTIONS: Read this poem about a hard-working blacksmith. Then answer questions 19 through 24. Darken the circle at the bottom of the page or write your answer on the lines.

The Village Blacksmith

by Henry Wadsworth Longfellow

Under a spreading chestnut tree
    The village **smithy** stands;
The smith, a mighty man is he,
    With large and sinewy hands;
And the muscles of his brawny arms
    Are strong as iron bands.

His hair is crisp, and black, and long,
    His face is like the tan;
His brow is wet with honest sweat,
    He earns whate'er he can,
And looks the whole world in the face,
    For he owes not any man.

Week in, week out, from morn till night,
    You can hear his **bellows** blow;
You can hear him swing his heavy **sledge,**
    With measured beat and slow,
Like a **sexton** ringing the village bell,
    When the evening sun is low.

smithy: workshop of a blacksmith
bellows: device for quickening a fire by blowing air on it
sledge: long, heavy hammer, usually held with both hands
sexton: church official in charge of ringing the bell

And children coming home from school
    Look in at the open door;
They love to see the flaming forge,
    And hear the bellows roar,
And catch the burning sparks that fly
    Like chaff from a threshing floor.

He goes on Sunday to the church,
    And sits among his boys;
He hears the parson pray and preach,
    He hears his daughter's voice,
Singing in the village choir,
    And it makes his heart rejoice.

It sounds to him like her mother's voice,
    Singing in Paradise!
He needs must think of her once more,
    How in the grave she lies;
And with his hard, rough hand he wipes
    A tear out of his eyes.

Toiling—rejoicing—sorrowing,
    Onward through life he goes;
Each morning sees some task begin,
    Each evening sees it close;
Something attempted, something done,
    Has earned a night's repose.

Thanks, thanks to thee, my worthy friend,
    For the lesson thou hast taught!
Thus at the flaming forge of life
    Our fortunes must be wrought;
Thus on its sounding anvil shaped
    Each burning deed and thought.

19 Why does his daughter's voice make the blacksmith's heart rejoice?

    F   He is proud of her beautiful voice.

    G   She is singing just for him.

    H   He loves her more than his other children.

    J   Her voice reminds him of his deceased wife.

Hint Identify details. The answer appears right in the poem. Use key words in the question to help you find it.

20 The lines, "And catch the burning sparks that fly / Like chaff from a threshing floor," are an example of—

    A   personification

    B   an idiom

    C   a simile

    D   a metaphor

Hint Personification gives human qualities to something that is not human. An idiom is a phrase whose meaning cannot be understood from the ordinary meanings of the words in it. A simile compares two unlike things using *like* or *as*. A metaphor speaks of one thing as if it were something else.

21 The author most likely wrote this poem to—

    F   describe the simple life of a blacksmith

    G   persuade readers to respect hard-working people

    H   convey a lesson found in the blacksmith's life

    J   explain the work that a blacksmith does

Hint Determine the author's purpose. Why do you think the author presents this account of the blacksmith's life?

Answers

19 Ⓕ Ⓖ Ⓗ Ⓙ	20 Ⓐ Ⓑ Ⓒ Ⓓ	21 Ⓕ Ⓖ Ⓗ Ⓙ

22 How does the blacksmith begin and end each day?

_____

_____

_____

_____

_____

_____

Hint Identify details. Look for the answer near the end of the poem

23 Longfellow often portrayed the values of the nineteenth-century American culture in his works. Give three values that you think the poem portrays. Use details from the poem to explain your answer.

_____

_____

_____

_____

_____

Hint Evaluate the poem. Think about the characteristics the blacksmith displays and the way he lives his life.

24   A character sketch is a description of someone's personality. It includes details and examples to show what he or she is like. Write a character sketch of the blacksmith.

Use a graphic organizer to plan your character sketch.

Draw a Character Traits Map to organize your thoughts about the blacksmith. Write a trait in each space coming off the center box. Then follow each trait to its "Event" box and write an event that illustrates that trait.

Write your character sketch on the lines below. If you need more space, continue writing on a separate sheet of paper.

_____

_____

_____

_____

_____

_____

_____

_____

_____

_____

_____

_____

_____

_____

Hint Determine character traits by identifying details from the poem. Look at the traits and events you wrote on the Character Traits Map. Do they give you a clear picture of what the blacksmith is like? Use this information to write your character sketch. Then remember to use the checklist on page 56 to review your writing.

This page may not be reproduced without permission of Steck-Vaughn/Berrent.

DIRECTIONS: Read these two selections by Mark Twain. The first is a story about an artist who rises to fame in a very unusual manner. The second is an excerpt from *The Adventures of Tom Sawyer*. Then answer questions 25 through 30. Darken the circle at the bottom of the page or write your answer on the lines.

Is He Living or Is He Dead?

by Mark Twain

I was spending the month of March, 1892, at Mentone, in the Riviera. At this restful spot, I got acquainted with a rich man. To disguise him I will call him Smith.

One day at our hotel, Smith exclaimed, "Quick! Cast your eye on the man going out the door." "Do you know who he is?"

"Yes. He is an old, retired, and very rich silk manufacturer. His name is Magnan."

I supposed that Smith would proceed to justify his interest in Magnan, but here we were interrupted. That evening I ran across Smith, and he asked me up to his cheerful parlor. After some lazy and contented conversation, he said, "Now I will tell a curious history. It has been a secret for many years—a secret between me and three others; I am going to break the seal now."

Here follows what he told me:

A long time ago I was a young artist, and I wandered about France, sketching here and there. I was presently joined by a couple of young Frenchmen, Claude and Carl, who were at the same kind of thing. We were as happy as we were poor.

An artist as poor as ourselves saved us from starving—François Millet. "What! The *great* François Millet?"

Great? He wasn't any greater than we were, then. He hadn't any fame, and he was so poor that he hadn't anything to feed us but turnips. We four became fast friends. We painted away, piling up stock, but very seldom getting rid of any of it.

For a little over two years this went on. At last, one day, Claude said, "Boys, I've been all around the village, and they refuse to credit us until all the odds and ends are paid up."

Every face was blank with dismay. Carl walked nervously up and down awhile, then said, "It's a shame! Look at these canvases. Aren't these pictures of very great and high merit? Of such great and high merit that, if an illustrious name were attached to them, they would sell at splendid prices. Isn't it so?"

"Certainly it is."

Carl sat down, and said, "Now, I have a perfectly serious thing to propose. I believe my project will make us all rich. The merit of many a great artist has never been acknowledged until after he was starved and dead. My project is this: we must cast lots—one of us must die."

There was a wild chorus of advice for the help of Carl's brain. He waited for us to calm down, then went on again with his project.

"Here's the idea. During the next three months the one who is to die shall paint sketches with all his might. The rest will be busy preparing for the coming event. When everything is just right, we'll spring the death on them. You get the idea?"

"Not quite."

"Don't you see? The man doesn't really die; he changes his name and vanishes; we bury a dummy, and cry over it, with all the world to help."

Everybody broke out into applause. We cast lots and Millet was elected to die. Next morning, the other three cleared out. Each of us carried a dozen of Millet's small pictures, purposing to market them. Carl struck for Paris, where he would start the work of building up Millet's fame. Claude and I were to scatter over France.

I sold one picture every day, and never tried to sell two. I always said to my customer, "I am a fool to sell a picture of Millet's at all, for that man is not going to live three months, and when he dies his pictures can't be had for love or money."

In Paris Carl made friends with the correspondents, and got Millet's condition reported to England and all over the continent, and America, and everywhere. After six weeks we three met in Paris and called a halt. Everything was so ripe that we saw that it would be a mistake not to strike now. So we wrote Millet to go to bed and begin to waste away pretty fast, for we should like him to die in ten days if he could get ready.

You remember the great funeral. We four carried the coffin, and would allow none to help. You see, we had substituted a light wax figure in place of a body.

"Which four?"

"*We* four—for Millet helped to carry his own coffin. In disguise, you know."

"Astonishing!"

"But true, just the same. Money? We didn't know what to do with it. And as for the sketches Millet shoveled out during the weeks we were on the road, well, it would astonish you to know the figure we sell them at nowadays."

"What became of Millet?"

"Do you remember the man I called your attention to today? *That was François Millet.*"

"Great—"

"Scott! Yes. For once they didn't starve a genius to death and then put into other pockets the rewards he should have had himself."

Tom Sawyer, Huckleberry Finn, and Joe Harper run away to Jackson's Island to become pirates. Meanwhile, their families plan a funeral service, thinking the boys are dead. The following excerpt tells what happens at the service.

from *The Adventures of Tom Sawyer*

by Mark Twain

It was a very still Sabbath. The villagers began to gather, loitering a moment in the vestibule to converse in whispers about the sad event. But there was no whispering in the house; only the funereal rustling of dresses as the women gathered to their seats, disturbed the silence there. There was finally a waiting pause, and expectant dumbness, and then Aunt Polly entered, followed by Sid and Mary, and they by the Harper family, all in deep black.

As the service proceeded, the clergyman drew such pictures of the graces, the winning ways and the rare promise of the lost lads, that every soul there thought he recognized these pictures. And each felt a pang in remembering that he had persistently blinded himself to them, always before, and had persistently seen only faults and flaws in the poor boys. The minister related many a touching incident in the lives of the departed, too, which illustrated their sweet, generous natures. The people could easily see, now, how noble and beautiful those episodes were, and remembered with grief that at the time they occurred they had seemed rank rascalities, well deserving of the cowhide. The congregation became more and more moved, as the pathetic tale went on, till at last the whole company broke down and joined the weeping mourners in a chorus of anguished sobs. The preacher himself gave way to his feelings and cried in the pulpit.

There was a rustle in the gallery, which nobody noticed; a moment later the church door creaked; the minister raised his streaming eyes above his handkerchief, and stood transfixed! First one and then another pair of eyes followed the minister's, and then almost with one impulse the congregation rose and stared while the three dead boys came marching up the aisle, Tom in the lead, Joe next, and Huck, a ruin of drooping rags, sneaking sheepishly in the rear! They had been hid in the unused gallery listening to their own funeral sermon!

This page may not be reproduced without permission of Steck-Vaughn/Berrent.

25 Why did the young artists in the first story come up with a scheme?

   A They were tired of eating turnips.

   B They could not get any more credit.

   C They were bored with their lives.

   D They wanted to be better painters.

   Hint Identify cause and effect relationships. Reread the part of the story just before Carl comes up with his plan.

26 How are François Millet and the boys (Tom, Joe, and Huck) alike?

   F They make a great deal of money after their "deaths."

   G They fake their deaths because they want to be pirates.

   H They want others to feel guilty for treating them badly.

   J They listen to what others say about them after they died.

   Hint Compare characters by making connections among the selections. Remember that the answer must pertain to both selections.

27 Mark Twain probably believed that—

   A people see only good in the dead

   B it is wrong to fake your death

   C mourners should always wear black

   D funerals are a waste of time and emotion

   Hint Understand the author's point of view. Consider what happens to the reputations of the "deceased" in both selections.

Answers

25 Ⓐ Ⓑ Ⓒ Ⓓ	26 Ⓕ Ⓖ Ⓗ Ⓙ	27 Ⓐ Ⓑ Ⓒ Ⓓ

28 Contrast the points of view used in both passages.

_____

_____

_____

_____

_____

_____

> **Hint** A story has a *first-person point of view* if the narrator is a part of the story. He or she is referred to as "I." A story has the *third-person point of view* if the narrator is not a part of the action of the story. The narrator refers to each character as "he" or "she" and tells the thoughts of all the characters.

29 How well do you think the title of the first passage, "Is He Living or Is He Dead?" would fit the second passage, the excerpt from *The Adventures of Tom Sawyer*? Use details and examples from the selection to support your response.

_____

_____

_____

_____

_____

_____

> **Hint** Make connections between the two selections and their main ideas. Think about what the excerpt from *The Adventures of Tom Sawyer* is about. Would the title convey the main idea of the piece?

30 What theme do the selections share? Trace this theme throughout one of the stories, explaining how it is revealed through plot, setting, and character.

Use a graphic organizer to plan your essay.

Think about how the messages of the two selections are similar. Then choose one selection to write about. Draw a Story Map. Write down the main parts of the selection. For the setting, you might not be able to tell exactly when and where the story takes place. Just write what you can about the setting.

Write your essay on the lines below. If you need more space, continue writing on a separate sheet of paper.

_____

_____

_____

_____

_____

_____

_____

_____

_____

_____

_____

_____

Hint Summarize the information and determine the theme for both selections. For your essay, first state the theme that the two selections share in common. Then look at the items you filled in on the Story Map. How do the elements help reveal the theme? Use this information to describe how the theme is developed in the passage. After you finish your essay, use the checklist on page 56 to make sure your writing is the best it can be.

Test

You will now be taking a practice test that includes all the skills you have reviewed in this book. Follow the directions in each section. As always, remember to use the **Four *R*s: R**eady, **R**ead, **R**espond, and **R**eview. You may look back at the reading passages as needed.

For the multiple-choice questions, work carefully and try to get as many questions right as you can. Do not spend too much time on any one question. If you are not sure of an answer, make the best choice you can and go on to the next question. You can go back and check answers later if you have time.

For the open-ended questions, plan out what you want to say before writing. Use graphic organizers to help you write your essays. Make sure that you respond to all parts of each item. After you finish writing, use the checklist on page 56 to help you review your work.

DIRECTIONS: Read this article about a man who followed his conscience and guided others to follow theirs. Then answer questions 1 through 11. Darken the circle on the separate answer sheet or write your answer on the lines.

Stand Like a Trumpet: The Story of John Woolman

by Deborah J. Rasmussen

Silence settled over the room. One by one, Friends nodded their approval, ending years of discord. In that moment, the New England yearly meeting of the Religious Society of Friends became the first major body of American Quakers to *abolish* slavery among its members. From that day in 1772, no one who bought, sold, or owned a slave in New England could claim to be a Friend. Ironically, John Woolman, the man who was largely responsible for this decision, had recently died while promoting antislavery far away in England.

John Woolman was born in New Jersey in 1720, the son of Quaker farmers. He learned Quaker ways and tried to live as Friends believed was right. When he was a child, he didn't find it easy to worship in attentive silence and oppose violence. But as he grew, young Woolman learned to listen to his conscience and to stand up for his beliefs.

Woolman loved the countryside around his boyhood home, but farm work didn't appeal to him. At the age of twenty, he moved to the town of Mount Holly to work as a store clerk and bookkeeper. The job went well until one day when his employer hurriedly asked him to write a bill of sale for some merchandise. That wasn't an unusual request, except that this time the "merchandise" was a black woman—a slave.

In that instant, Woolman knew for certain that slavery was wrong. But the sale had come up suddenly, and the buyer, a Quaker, was waiting. Woolman didn't want to trouble a respected member of his own religion. And he knew his duty to his employer: to do as he was told. But to *sell* a fellow human being?

John Woolman obeyed his employer that day. He tried to quiet his troubled conscience by stating then and there that he believed slavery was wrong. It didn't help. He deeply regretted his role in the transaction. Never again would he participate in a slave sale. But that wasn't enough. Woolman knew he had to do something more about slavery.

Woolman wasn't the first Quaker to oppose slavery. Several had openly objected to the practice. But in those days, most Quakers had never thought of slavery as wrong. Many participated in the slave trade, and those who owned slaves treated them well. They resented the blunt criticism of the few who denounced slavery. So the first

Friends to favor abolition of slavery were largely ignored. Some were treated harshly—even thrown out of their local congregations, or meetings.

John Woolman was different. He opposed slavery but didn't criticize slave owners. He believed that if they heard the truth and listened to their consciences, they would see for themselves that slavery was wrong. Only then would they change. Woolman told his own meeting how he felt. Then he began to travel around the Colonies. He met with large Quaker groups and with individuals. He visited Quaker families–including those with slaves—in their homes. After witnessing the hard work slaves did for nothing, Woolman never again accepted their free service. He carried silver coins to pay black men and women for their labor and used the opportunity to explain his feelings to their surprised owners.

Almost no one changed instantly because of Woolman's visits. Quakers voiced many reasons for keeping slaves. Tribal life in Africa was difficult and dangerous, they pointed out. Blacks were better off in America, especially in Quaker homes. If slaves were freed, Friends argued, they couldn't support themselves and would end up enslaved by someone else, maybe someone less kind. Besides, slave labor would be hard to replace. Quaker families might lose their farms and businesses. Even Friends who agreed that slavery was wrong argued that it couldn't end immediately. Everyone needed more time.

Woolman listened. Giving up slavery would be hard, he agreed. He felt compassion for slave and slave owner alike. But slavery was still wrong. Woolman reminded Friends that no person willingly became a slave. If blacks were brought to America for a better life, he asserted, they should live as freely as whites. Instead, they labored while white slave owners grew rich and idle. That, Woolman insisted, was harmful to all. The time to end slavery had come. More time meant more injustice. Friends would have to help each other as well as the freed slaves to make a life without slavery succeed.

It was hard for many Quakers to accept Woolman's words. But his approach was kind and patient, his message full of concern for all. He was respected everywhere he went; even those who disagreed with him weren't offended. He was never thrown out of his religious community. And the more Woolman spoke, the more Friends listened and changed. Some freed their slaves, while others spoke up, following Woolman's example. Eventually every Quaker meeting in America was questioning the practice of slavery. But Friends require unity to make group decisions. Before a meeting could forbid slavery among its members, each Friend had to approve, based on his or her own conscience. Because many prominent Friends of Woolman's time owned slaves, it took years to achieve unity about abolition.

These were hard years for Woolman. Travel was slow and tiring. He was often far from his wife and daughter, sometimes spending uncomfortable nights on the road. He deplored the ongoing practice of slavery, grieved for slaves who would never see freedom and for slave owners whose hearts were closed. He worried about white children growing up idle and spoiled while black children and adults did all the work. He felt a growing gloom over the country and feared that future generations would suffer because of slavery. But he never gave up.

John Woolman didn't live to see slavery abolished, but he did see the beginnings of change among Quakers. At the end of the eighteenth century, The Society of Friends became the first religious body in America to abolish slavery among all its members. Soon it also became the first to advocate abolition as state and national policy. In the troubled years leading to the Civil War, Friends were active in the antislavery movement, the Underground Railroad, and the welfare and education of freed slaves. It wasn't easy, but Quakers had learned from John Woolman to "stand like a trumpet," proclaiming what their consciences said was right. And so they stood, until slavery was abolished in America once and for all.

1 In this article, the word *abolish* means—

    A reflect on

    B argue for

    C put restrictions on

    D do away with

2 The title of this passage is an example of—

    F a simile

    G an idiom

    H a metaphor

    J an analogy

3 Which of the following does *not* support the author's assertion that Woolman was respected everywhere he went?

    A People who disagreed with him were not offended.

    B He was never thrown out of his religious community.

    C The more he spoke, the more Friends listened and changed.

    D Quakers gave him many reasons for keeping slaves.

4 Which of the following *best* states the author's attitude toward John Woolman?

    F He was too reckless in his anti-slavery endeavors.

    G He should be admired for his patience and persistence.

    H He was too meek to sway people to his point of view.

    J He should be applauded for achieving his goal during his lifetime.

5 Why did it take years for the Quakers to agree that they should give up slavery?

  A They found it difficult to agree on any issue.

  B Not enough members spoke out against slavery.

  C They were worried that some families might lose their farms.

  D They believed the slaves wanted to work for them.

6 Which is an *opinion* from the article?

  F John Woolman obeyed his employer that day.

  G The time to end slavery had come.

  H Almost no one changed instantly because of Woolman's visits.

  J He met with large Quaker groups and with individuals.

7 Which of the following was an argument used by John Woolman to support his position?

  A It would take many years to end slavery.

  B Tribal life in Africa was difficult and dangerous.

  C White slave owners and their children were growing idle.

  D Slaves were incapable of supporting themselves.

8 If you wanted to find out more about John Woolman, you should—

  F go to a Quaker meeting

  G look up *Woolman* in a dictionary

  H look in an encyclopedia under "Quakers"

  J read a biography about him

9   What incident caused John Woolman to speak out against slavery?

_____

_____

_____

_____

_____

_____

10   What would be another good title for this article? Explain your choice.

_____

_____

_____

_____

_____

_____

❚❚   Trace John Woolman's impact on the abolitionist movement among Quakers. Why was John Woolman able to sway the opinion of the Friends? What resulted because of this?

Use a graphic organizer to plan your essay.

Write your essay on the lines below. If you need more space, continue writing on a separate sheet of paper.

_____

_____

_____

_____

_____

_____

_____

_____

_____

_____

_____

_____

_____

DIRECTIONS: Read this story about a murderer who cannot turn off his conscience. Then answer questions 12 through 22. Darken the circle on the separate answer sheet or write your answer on the lines.

The Tell-Tale Heart

by Edgar Allan Poe

True!—nervous—very, very dreadfully nervous I had been and am; but why *will* you say that I am a madman? The disease had sharpened my five senses—not destroyed—not dulled them. Listen, and see how lucidly—how calmly I can tell you the whole story.

It is impossible to say how the idea first entered my brain; but once conceived, it haunted me day and night. There was no good reason. There was no real hatred. I loved the old man. He had never done me any wrong. For his gold I had no desire. I think it was his eye! Yes, it was this! One of his eyes looked like a vulture's—a pale blue eye, with a film over it. Whenever it fell upon me, my blood ran cold; and so—very gradually—I made up my mind to take his life, and thus get rid of that eye forever.

You should have seen how wisely I proceeded. I was never kinder to the old man than during the whole week before I killed him. And every night, about midnight, I turned the knob of his door and opened it—oh, so gently! I put in a dark lantern, and then I slowly put in my head. And then, when my head was well in the room, I undid the lantern just so much that a single thin ray fell upon the vulture eye. And this I did for seven long nights—every night just at midnight—but I found the eye always closed; and so it was impossible to do the work; for it was not the old man who vexed me, but his Evil Eye.

On the eighth night, I was about to open the lantern, when my thumb slipped on the tin, and the old man sprang up in the bed crying out—"Who's there?"

I kept quite still and said nothing. For a whole hour I did not move a muscle, and in the meantime I did not hear him lie down. He was still sitting up in the bed, listening.

In a little while I heard a slight groan, and I knew it was the groan of mortal terror. Death, in approaching him, had stalked with his black shadow before him, and enveloped the victim. And it was the unperceived shadow that caused him to *feel* the presence of my head within the room.

When I had waited a long time, very patiently, without hearing him lie down, I opened a little crevice in the lantern until a single dim ray, like the thread of a spider, shot out from the crack and full upon the vulture eye.

It was open—wide, wide open—and I grew furious as I looked upon it. I saw it so clearly—all a dull blue, with a hideous veil over it that chilled my very bones.

There came to my ears a low, dull, quick sound, such as a watch makes when enveloped in cotton. I knew *that* sound well, too. It was the beating of the old man's heart.

I scarcely breathed. I held the lantern motionless. The hellish drumbeat of the heart grew quicker and quicker, and louder and louder every instant. The old man's terror *must* have been great! I thought the heart must burst. And now a new anxiety seized me—the sound would be heard by a neighbor! The old man's hour had come! With a loud yell, I threw open the lantern and leaped into the room. He shrieked loudly once—once only. In an instant I dragged him to the floor, and pulled the heavy bed over him. For many minutes, the heart beat on with a muffled sound. At length it ceased. The old man was dead. His eye would trouble me no more.

I then took up three planks from the floor of the chamber and deposited all underneath. I then replaced the boards so cleverly that no human eye could have noticed anything wrong.

When I had finished, it was four o'clock. As the bell sounded the hour, there came a knocking at the street door. Three policemen entered. A shriek had been heard by a neighbor during the night; suspicion of foul play had been aroused. The officers had been appointed to search the premises.

I smiled—for *what* had I to fear? The shriek, I said, was my own in a dream. The old man, I mentioned, was absent in the country. I took my visitors all over the house. I let them search—search *well*. I led them, at length, to *his* chamber. I showed them his treasures, secure, undisturbed. I brought chairs into the room and desired them *here* to rest.

The officers were satisfied. My *manner* had convinced them. They sat, and while I answered cheerily, they talked about familiar things. But, before long, I felt myself getting pale and wished them gone. My head ached, and I fancied a ringing in my ears. The ringing became more distinct until, at length, I found that the noise was *not* within my ears.

No doubt I now grew *very* pale—but I talked more fluently and with a heightened voice. Yet the sound increased—and what could I do?

It was *a low, dull, quick sound—much such a sound as a watch makes when enveloped in cotton*. I gasped for breath—and yet the officers heard it not. I talked more quickly—more forcefully; but the noise steadily increased. I argued about trifles, in a high key and with violent waving of the arms, but the noise steadily increased. Why *would* they not be gone? I paced the floor with heavy strides. I swung the chair upon which I had been sitting

and grated it upon the boards, but the noise arose over all and continually increased. It grew louder—louder—*louder*! And still the men chatted pleasantly and smiled. Was it possible they did not hear it? No, no! They heard!—they suspected!—they *knew*!—they were making a mockery of my horror! I could bear those knowing smiles no longer! I felt that I must scream or die!—and now—again!—listen! louder! louder! louder! *louder*!—

"Villains!" I shrieked, "pretend no more! I admit the deed!—tear up the planks!—here, here!—it is the beating of his hideous heart!"

12 Why does the narrator decide to kill the old man?

 A   He wants to get the old man's gold.

 B   The old man is cruel to him.

 C   He wants to get rid of the Evil Eye.

 D   He is jealous of the old man.

13 The narrator is probably telling the story from—

 F   his room in the house

 G   a mental hospital or prison

 H   the old man's room

 J   a friend's house

14 The boxes show some things that happen in the story.

The narrator wakes up the old man.		The narrator kills the old man.
1	2	3

Which event belongs in Box 2?

 A   The narrator takes up three planks from the floor.

 B   The police arrive at the old man's door.

 C   The narrator brings chairs into the old man's room.

 D   The narrator leaps into the old man's room.

15 Why does the narrator enter the old man's room on seven previous nights before finally killing him?

 F   He wants to wait until the old man's eye is open.

 G   He wants to make the old man think he is crazy.

 H   He wants to wait until the old man is alone.

 J   He wants to make sure the old man is sound asleep.

16 The mood of this story is one of—

   A horror

   B romance

   C anger

   D despair

17 From the story, you can infer that—

   F the old man really does have an Evil Eye

   G the old man really does not shriek loudly when the narrator attacks him

   H the narrator does not really bury the body under the floor

   J the old man's heart does not really beat loudly when the police arrive

18 The sentence, "Death, in approaching him, had stalked with his black shadow before him, and enveloped the victim," is an example of—

   A a simile

   B hyperbole

   C personification

   D a metaphor

19 Which of the following *best* tells the theme of the story?

   F A guilty conscience can drive a person crazy.

   G A guilty conscience will haunt a person.

   H You can tell a lot about people by looking at their eyes.

   J The truth is often the best defense.

20   From which point of view is the story told? Why is this point of view
particularly effective for this story?

_____

_____

_____

_____

_____

21   What finally causes the narrator to confess?

_____

_____

_____

_____

_____

22   At the beginning of the story, the narrator says that he is not mad. Imagine
that you are a psychiatrist asked to write a report for the court on the
narrator's sanity. Decide whether or not you believe the narrator is mad.
Then write your report, citing specific character traits and events to support
your opinion.

Use a graphic organizer to plan your report.

Write your report on the lines below. If you need more space, continue writing on a separate sheet of paper.

_____

_____

_____

_____

_____

_____

_____

_____

_____

_____

_____

_____

_____

_____

_____

_____

DIRECTIONS: Read this article about the flag that inspired our National Anthem. Then answer questions 23 through 33. Darken the circle on the separate answer sheet or write your answer on the lines.

Star-Spangled Seamstress

by Lynn E. McElfresh

It started with a snip, then a cut, and then stitch after tiny stitch. Caroline Pickersgill was thirteen years old when she began the largest sewing project of her life. It was the summer of 1813. She had no idea that the finished product would inspire a song Americans know by heart.

Caroline learned how to sew from her mother, a widow who was a "maker of colours," as flag makers were called at the time. Like Caroline, Mrs. Pickersgill had learned how to make flags from her mother. Rebecca Young, Caroline's grandmother, had made flags for the Continental Army during the American Revolution. The three women were a family of flag makers.

America was at war with the British again in the summer of 1813. The British navy was attacking towns up and down the Atlantic coast. Rumors spread that the British would attack Baltimore, where the family of flag makers lived at 60 Albemarle Street. Early in July, two officers from nearby Fort McHenry knocked at their door. Major George Armistead, the fort's commander, wanted the Pickersgills to sew a flag so big that "the British will have no difficulty in seeing it from a distance."

A photograph of the flag taken in the 1870s

Immediately, the family of flag makers began to work on the huge banner. They gathered materials: four hundred yards of red, white, and blue English wool bunting, and white American cotton for the stars. Next, they cut. Caroline and her mother snipped fifteen stars. Each measured two feet from point to point. They cut and sewed eight red and seven white stripes, each two feet wide.

When it came time to stitch the flag together, they had a problem. No room in their house was big enough to lay out a flag so large. Caroline and her mother asked the owner of a brewery down the street if they could spread the flag on the malt-house floor after the brewery closed for the evening. Night after night, Caroline, her mother, and her grandmother worked by candlelight. Using linen thread, they joined the stars and stripes with small, tight stitches. After six weeks of snipping and stitching, the finished flag measured thirty feet by forty-two feet. Hung lengthwise, it was as tall as a four-story building.

Soldiers from Fort McHenry picked up the flag from Mrs. Pickersgill on August 13, 1813. The flag makers were paid $405.90 for their efforts. (Many of the men who worked along the docks didn't earn that sum in a year.) The flag Caroline had worked so frantically to finish was put into storage as the men waited and prepared for the British. It would be more than a year before the flag would be hoisted over the garrison.

On August 19, 1814, the British fleet entered Chesapeake Bay. Their first target was the capital city, Washington. The night of August 24, Caroline saw the glow of flames on the horizon as Washington burned forty miles away. Would Baltimore be next?

Early in the morning of September 13, British ships turned their attention to Fort McHenry. The star-shaped fort was all that stood between the city of Baltimore and the British fleet. Into the rainy night, the British fired 1500 bombs and Congreve rockets at the fort. Fiery red arcs blazed across the sky. Explosions mixed with thunder. All night, Baltimore shook with the sounds of war.

Two hours before dawn, an eerie silence settled over the harbor. No bombs burst. No rockets glared. What did the silence mean? Was the battle over? Had Fort McHenry surrendered? All of Baltimore wondered as they waited for dawn.

Francis Scott Key wondered, too. Key was a Washington lawyer and amateur poet waiting aboard a ship eight miles from the Baltimore harbor. After the burning of Washington, Key visited the British fleet anchored in Chesapeake Bay to ask for the release of a friend held prisoner there. While successful in his mission, Key was *detained* at sea by the British.

Using a spyglass, Key searched the dawn sky until he saw what he had been hoping for. Caroline's banner—the great red, white, and blue flag—was proudly waving in the breeze above Fort McHenry! The British had given up. The fort and Baltimore had been saved.

Sometime before dawn the rain-soaked storm flag had been lowered, and the great new flag had been hoisted for the British fleet to see as they sailed from the harbor. The sight of the flag inspired Key to write a poem that was soon set to music. A month later, a Baltimore actor who sang Key's new song in a public performance called it "The Star-Spangled Banner."

In 1931, "The Star-Spangled Banner" officially became our National Anthem. Today, the banner Caroline helped to stitch—the fifteen-star-and-fifteen-stripe flag that inspired Francis Scott Key—is at the Smithsonian's National Museum of American History in Washington, D.C., where it is being restored.

23 Why did Major Armistead want the flag to be so big?

 A He wanted it to inspire soldiers to fight harder.

 B He wanted the British to be able to see it from a distance.

 C He thought the British would have trouble taking it down.

 D He wanted it to hide the entrance to Fort McHenry.

24 Why did the author include the fact that the flag makers made more money than many of the dock workers earned in a year?

 F She wanted to suggest that the flag makers were overpaid.

 G She wanted to add an interesting aside.

 H She wanted to indicate how much the flag makers' work was valued.

 J She wanted to protest the low pay of the dock workers.

25 Another good title for this article is—

 A "The Pickersgill Women"

 B "Francis Scott Key: Lawyer and Songwriter"

 C "The Battle for Baltimore"

 D "The Flag that Inspired Our Anthem"

26 There is enough information in this article to show that if the British had taken Baltimore—

 F "The Star-Spangled Banner" would not have been written

 G Francis Scott Key would have been arrested

 H the United States could never have won the War of 1812

 J the Pickersgill family would have been tried for treason

27 You can tell that *detained* means—

    A delayed

    B searched

    C recruited

    D entertained

28 Why was the flag put in storage for over a year?

    F Major Armistead changed his mind about using the flag.

    G The flag was unfinished.

    H The British did not attack Fort McHenry until September of 1814.

    J Major Armistead wanted to keep the flag a secret.

29 Which word *best* describes how Francis Scott Key felt when he saw the flag?

    A relieved

    B confused

    C troubled

    D excited

30 To find out more about the War of 1812, you should—

    F read a biography of Francis Scott Key

    G look in an encyclopedia under "War of 1812"

    H consult an atlas for a map of the United States in the 1800s

    J search on the Internet using the key word *warfare*

31 What did Caroline Pickersgill and Francis Scott Key have in common?

_____

_____

_____

_____

_____

32 How does this article differ from material you might find in a history textbook?

_____

_____

_____

_____

_____

33 Imagine that you are Caroline Pickersgill. In a letter to a friend, describe your role in making the flag, your feelings about it, and your opinion of the song that was inspired by the flag.

Use a graphic organizer to plan your letter.

Write your letter on the lines below. If you need more space, continue writing on a separate sheet of paper.

DIRECTIONS: Read this poem about an abandoned house. Then answer questions 34 through 44. Darken the circle on the separate answer sheet or write your answer on the lines.

The House with Nobody in It

by Joyce Kilmer

Whenever I walk to Suffern along the Erie track,

I go by a poor old farmhouse with its shingles broken and black.

I suppose I've passed it a hundred times, but I always stop for a minute,

And look at the house, the tragic house, the house with nobody in it.

I never have seen a haunted house, but I hear there are such things;

That they hold the talk of spirits, their *mirth* and sorrowings.

I know this house isn't haunted, and I wish it were, I do;

For it wouldn't be so lonely if it had a ghost or two.

This house on the road to Suffern needs a dozen panes of glass,

And somebody ought to weed the walk and take a scythe to the grass.

It needs new paint and shingles, and the vines should be trimmed and tied;

But what it needs the most of all is some people living inside.

If I had a lot of money and all my debts were paid,

I'd put a gang of men to work with brush and saw and spade.

I'd buy that place and fix it up the way it used to be

And I'd find some people who wanted a home and give it to them free.

Now, a new house standing empty, with staring window and door,

Looks idle, perhaps, and foolish, like a hat on its block in the store.

But there's nothing mournful about it; it cannot be sad and lone

For the lack of something within it that it has never known.

But a house that has done what a house should do, a house that has sheltered life,

That has put its loving wooden arms around a man and his wife,

A house that has echoed a baby's laugh and held up his stumbling feet,

Is the saddest sight, when it's left alone, that ever your eyes could meet.

So whenever I go to Suffern along the Erie track,

I never go by the empty house without stopping and looking back,

Yet it hurts me to look at the crumbling roof and the shutters fallen apart,

For I can't help thinking the poor old house is a house with a broken heart.

34 Why does the speaker stop to look at the abandoned farmhouse?

   A He likes the way the house looks.

   B He knew the people who lived there.

   C He is thinking of buying it.

   D He feels sorry for it.

35 Another word for *mirth* is—

   F joyfulness

   G grieving

   H rage

   J alarm

36 According to the poem, why can't "a new house standing empty" be mournful?

   A It has never had a family living inside.

   B Everything in it is clean and new.

   C It holds the talk of spirits.

   D It has a great deal to look forward to.

37 You can tell that this is a poem and not another literary form because it—

   F has similes

   G lacks dialogue

   H rhymes

   J uses metaphor

38   The lines, "But a house that has done what a house should do, / a house that has sheltered life, / That has put its loving wooden arms around a man and his wife," are an example of—

A   a metaphor

B   personification

C   an analogy

D   a simile

39   What is the mood of the poem?

F   suspenseful

G   playful

H   mournful

J   fearful

40   What would be another good title for this poem?

A   "Along the Erie Track"

B   "Sheltering Life"

C   "Stopping to Look Back"

D   "The Tragic Farmhouse"

41   The author probably wrote this poem to—

F   describe an old farmhouse along the Erie track

G   persuade the reader to buy an abandoned house

H   inform the reader about different kinds of houses

J   share his feelings about an abandoned farmhouse

42   Explain the theme of the poem.

_____

_____

_____

_____

_____

_____

43   What can you tell about the speaker of the poem?

_____

_____

_____

_____

_____

_____

44 Compare and contrast "the house with nobody in it" with other houses mentioned in the poem. Do you agree with the author that it is the most tragic house of all? Why or why not?

Use a graphic organizer to plan your essay.

Write your essay on the lines below. If you need more space, continue writing on a separate sheet of paper.

_____

_____

_____

_____

_____

_____

_____

_____

_____

_____

_____

_____

_____

_____

_____

_____

_____

DIRECTIONS: First read the article about a train that runs by magnetic power. Next read the list of advantages to using such a train. Then answer questions 45 through 55. Darken the circle on the separate answer sheet or write your answer on the lines.

Flying Trains

by Pam Daniels

How would you like to fly in a train? You can, you know. You can ride a jet without wings and race to your destination, never leaving the ground. All you need is a *maglev*, a train that runs by magnetic *levitation*.

Each end of a magnet is called a polarity and is either positive or negative. When the positive ends of two magnets come close together, they push away from each other, because magnets of like polarity repel. But if you turn one of those magnets around so that its positive end gets close to the other's negative side, both magnets will slam together—magnets of opposite polarities attract. And if you keep turning one of the magnets back and forth to repel and then attract, you'll create a wave of magnetic current.

A maglev train uses these principles to surf the magnetic wave. There are powerful magnets in both the train and the single, elevated guideway it rests on. First these magnets work together, raising the fifty-ton train slightly above the guideway to float on a cushion of air. Then the train's magnets switch back and forth between positive and negative polarities, creating a strong magnetic wave alongside the maglev. This wave locks into the guideway's own magnetic current, and the two waves combine to push and pull the train along. Using magnetic power ensures that maglev trains are silent, except for the *whoosh* they make outside as they pass. Inside, there's no engine roar and no other sounds—or sensations—of motion.

A maglev's shape is aerodynamic. There are no parts sticking out to block the wind that flows over and around the flying train, and it looks like a bullet or a plane without wings. And this train truly does fly. It can travel through the air at more than 250 miles per hour! Regular trains can go no faster than 130 miles per hour, and only on very straight tracks. But a maglev's guideway can curve many times without slowing the train, because a maglev's bottom surface wraps around the guide rail to keep the train from falling off.

There are no maglevs in the United States, and to ride one, you'd have to travel to Japan or Germany. Japan's maglev is called the *Shinkansen*, which means "bullet train." Over one million people ride 320 miles on it from Tokyo to Osaka every day. This trip used to take more than four hours, but it takes the bullet train only two and a half. Germany's maglev is called the Trans Rapid. It travels between four major cities, gliding along a magnetic guideway twenty-three feet above ground level.

ADVANTAGES OF MAGLEV

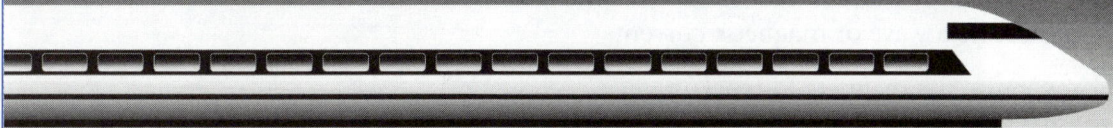

Magnetic Fields

► The intensity of magnetic field effects of a maglev is very low.

► Common household devices produce stronger magnetic fields than a maglev does.

Noise Levels

► Typical city traffic produces more noise than a maglev.

► A maglev's vibrations are not perceptible by humans.

Power Failure

► Batteries on board are activated to bring the train to the next station.

► The batteries are continually charged.

Safety

► A maglev is 20 times safer than an airplane, 250 times safer than other types of trains, and 700 times safer than road travel.

► Collision is unlikely because only sections of the track are activated as necessary.

Operation Costs

► There is no maintenance. The main cause of mechanical wear is friction. Because magnetic levitation requires no contact, there is no friction.

► A maglev uses 30% less energy than a high-speed train traveling at the same speed. You get $1/3$ more power for the same amount of energy.

45   In the article, *levitation* means—

   A   speed

   B   movement

   C   boost

   D   fields

46   What occurs if you keep turning one of a pair of magnets back and forth?

   F   You create a wave of magnetic current.

   G   You cause the magnets to repel.

   H   You cause the magnets to slam together.

   J   You cause the magnets to lift off the ground.

47   Why does a maglev train make curves easily?

   A   There are no parts sticking out to block the wind that flows over and around the train.

   B   Its magnets create a strong magnetic wave that locks into the guideway's own magnetic current.

   C   Its bottom surface wraps around the guide rail to keep the train from falling off.

   D   Only sections of the train's track are activated as necessary.

48   There is enough information in the article to infer that—

   F   maglev trains cost more to build than conventional trains

   G   Germany and Japan are behind the United States when it comes to technology in transportation

   H   magnetic energy is not as powerful as other forms of energy

   J   maglev trains provide a comfortable ride for passengers

This page may not be reproduced without permission of Steck-Vaughn/Berrent.

49 The author of the second selection included the information on magnetic fields to—

    A present interesting facts that might hold the reader's attention

    B calm any fears about the negative effects of maglev's magnetic fields

    C inform readers about the advantages of maglev trains

    D warn readers to use household devices only when necessary

50 Under which section in the second selection could you list the fact that a maglev has no moving parts to wear out?

    F Magnetic Fields

    G Noise Levels

    H Safety

    J Operation Costs

51 What happens if the magnetic power fails on a maglev?

    A Batteries are activated to bring the train to the next station.

    B Emergency backup magnets are used.

    C A regular train is sent in to tow the maglev to the next station.

    D The train automatically begins to run on backup electric power.

52 Which of the following statements from the second selection needs supporting evidence the *most*?

    F Maglev's vibrations are not perceptible by humans.

    G Maglev is 20 times safer than an airplane, 250 times safer than other types of trains, and 700 times safer than road travel.

    H Because magnetic levitation requires no contact, there is no friction.

    J Maglev uses 30% less energy that a high-speed train traveling at the same speed.

53   Describe three ways that a maglev train is different from a regular train.

_____

_____

_____

_____

_____

_____

54   Explain the differences in purpose between the two selections.

_____

_____

_____

_____

_____

_____

55 Suppose that you are on a debating team arguing that funding should be spent in your state to build a maglev. Write your presentation, using information from both selections to make your case.

Use a graphic organizer to plan your presentation.

Write your presentation on the lines below. If you need more space, continue writing on a separate sheet of paper.

_____

_____

_____

_____

_____

_____

_____

_____

_____

_____

_____

_____

_____

_____

_____

_____

Answer Sheet

STUDENT'S NAME			SCHOOL:

LAST | **FIRST** | **MI** | **TEACHER:**

FEMALE ○ MALE ○

Birth Date

MONTH	DAY	YEAR
Jan ○	⓪ ⓪	⑦ ⓪
Feb ○	① ①	⑧ ①
Mar ○	② ②	⑨ ②
Apr ○	③ ③	⓪ ③
May ○	④	④
Jun ○	⑤	⑤
Jul ○	⑥	⑥
Aug ○	⑦	⑦
Sep ○	⑧	⑧
Oct ○	⑨	⑨
Nov ○		
Dec ○		

GRADE ⑥ ⑦ ⑧ ⑨ ⑩ ⑪

Reading & Writing Excellence

Level G

TEST

1 Ⓐ Ⓑ Ⓒ Ⓓ	11 essay	21 short-answer	31 short-answer	41 Ⓕ Ⓖ Ⓗ Ⓙ	51 Ⓐ Ⓑ Ⓒ Ⓓ
2 Ⓕ Ⓖ Ⓗ Ⓙ	12 Ⓐ Ⓑ Ⓒ Ⓓ	22 essay	32 short-answer	42 short-answer	52 Ⓕ Ⓖ Ⓗ Ⓙ
3 Ⓐ Ⓑ Ⓒ Ⓓ	13 Ⓕ Ⓖ Ⓗ Ⓙ	23 Ⓐ Ⓑ Ⓒ Ⓓ	33 essay	43 short-answer	53 short-answer
4 Ⓕ Ⓖ Ⓗ Ⓙ	14 Ⓐ Ⓑ Ⓒ Ⓓ	24 Ⓕ Ⓖ Ⓗ Ⓙ	34 Ⓐ Ⓑ Ⓒ Ⓓ	44 essay	54 short-answer
5 Ⓐ Ⓑ Ⓒ Ⓓ	15 Ⓕ Ⓖ Ⓗ Ⓙ	25 Ⓐ Ⓑ Ⓒ Ⓓ	35 Ⓕ Ⓖ Ⓗ Ⓙ	45 Ⓐ Ⓑ Ⓒ Ⓓ	55 essay
6 Ⓕ Ⓖ Ⓗ Ⓙ	16 Ⓐ Ⓑ Ⓒ Ⓓ	26 Ⓕ Ⓖ Ⓗ Ⓙ	36 Ⓐ Ⓑ Ⓒ Ⓓ	46 Ⓕ Ⓖ Ⓗ Ⓙ	
7 Ⓐ Ⓑ Ⓒ Ⓓ	17 Ⓕ Ⓖ Ⓗ Ⓙ	27 Ⓐ Ⓑ Ⓒ Ⓓ	37 Ⓕ Ⓖ Ⓗ Ⓙ	47 Ⓐ Ⓑ Ⓒ Ⓓ	
8 Ⓕ Ⓖ Ⓗ Ⓙ	18 Ⓐ Ⓑ Ⓒ Ⓓ	28 Ⓕ Ⓖ Ⓗ Ⓙ	38 Ⓐ Ⓑ Ⓒ Ⓓ	48 Ⓕ Ⓖ Ⓗ Ⓙ	
9 short-answer	19 Ⓕ Ⓖ Ⓗ Ⓙ	29 Ⓐ Ⓑ Ⓒ Ⓓ	39 Ⓕ Ⓖ Ⓗ Ⓙ	49 Ⓐ Ⓑ Ⓒ Ⓓ	
10 short-answer	20 short-answer	30 Ⓕ Ⓖ Ⓗ Ⓙ	40 Ⓐ Ⓑ Ⓒ Ⓓ	50 Ⓕ Ⓖ Ⓗ Ⓙ	